Gay
Planet

Gay Planet

ALL THINGS
FOR ALL
(GAY)
MEN

Eric Chaline

ST. MARTIN'S PRESS
NEW YORK

CONTENTS

ISBN: 0-312-25322-2

First U.S. Edition: June 2000

10 9 8 7 6 5 4 3 2 1

Conceived, designed, and produced by
Quarto Publishing plc
The Old Brewery
6 Blundell Street
London N7 9BH

QUAR.TPA

Project editors: Michelle Pickering, Anna Watson
Senior art editor: Elizabeth Healey
Copy editors: Casey Horton, Hilary Sagar
Designer: Julie Francis
Photographer: Rosa Rodrigo
Illustrator: Peter Mundy
Picture researcher: Laurent Boubounelle
Indexer: Dorothy Frame

Art director: Moira Clinch
Publisher: Piers Spence

Printed & Manufactured by Regent Publishing Services Ltd, Hong Kong

INTRODUCTION

On the eve of the new millennium, in 1999, the gay community celebrated the 30th anniversary of the Stonewall Riots, the event that marked the beginning of the Gay Liberation movement in the developed world. In the decades that have passed since that fateful day of June 28th, 1969, we have come out of the closet as a community, transforming both ourselves and society. In the 1970s, gay ghettos were created as safe havens during the early years of struggle and search for a gay identity. The 1980s brought the tragedy of HIV-AIDS. However, the gay community's response to the epidemic ultimately made it stronger and better organized, and gave it unparalleled visibility. The 1990s were a time of healing and excess – a giant sigh of relief that the worst prophecies of the doom-mongers had been proved wrong. Today, in the first years of the 21st century, full integration in the developed world is no longer a far-off dream but a reality within our grasp.

The young gay men coming of age in the 21st century are self-confident and positive. They have the means to realize their expectations: they are enfranchised in the political process and courted as corporate consumers. This book is dedicated to them, to tell them where they have come from, and what they can make of their world.

SISTERS IN THE STRUGGLE

The male emphasis of this book is in no way intended to belittle the contribution of lesbians and transgendered people to the liberation struggle and gay life during the past 30 years. However, it is a fact that in many areas of their lives, these three communities have chosen to develop separately. Companion volumes, covering lesbian and transgendered people's lifestyles and cultures, await the pens of much better qualified authors.

FLAG WAVING

The rainbow flag, once a symbol of solidarity in struggle, is now, for the gays of the developed world, a symbol of solidarity in celebration.

As it was then,
how it is now

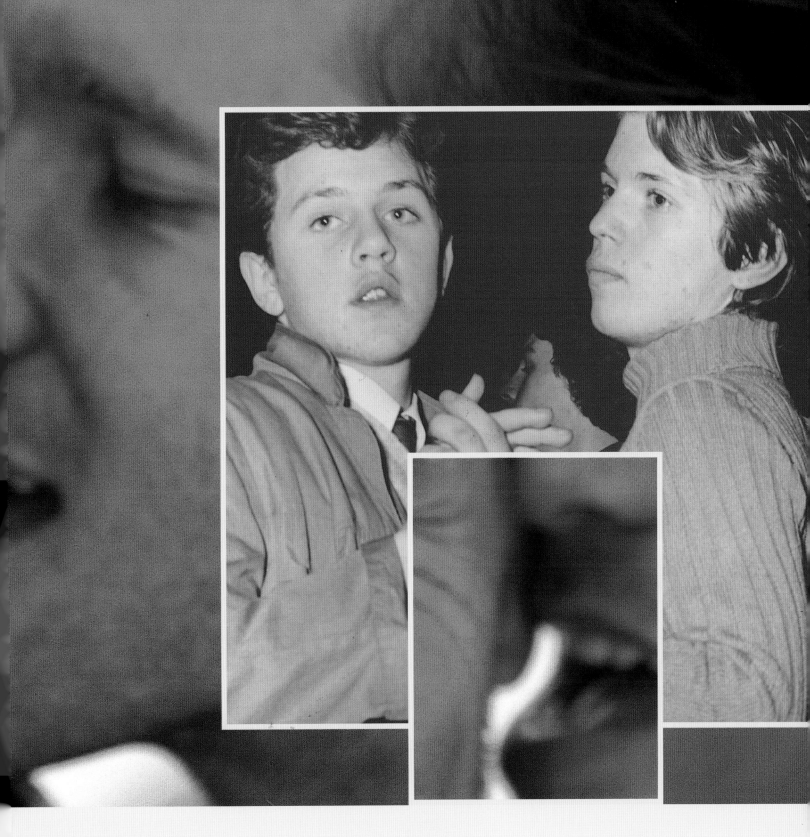

I f anyone had sat down to write a book celebrating all things gay and male in 1969, the result would have been very different. The section dealing with the present, "We are everywhere," would have consisted of police reports of "criminal" homosexual activity in the developed world, and anthropological studies of same-sex experiences in non-Western cultures. In order to find positive images of gay life, the only option would have been to expand the historical section, "Gays past," in order to look back to more tolerant times.

GAYS PAST

Love and sex between men has always been part of the human experience, but the way homosexuality has been understood by any given culture and by the men involved has varied widely with time and place. Although we have no archeological evidence of sexuality during the prehistoric period, it is possible to draw limited conclusions from anthropological studies of pre-industrial cultures that survived into the modern period, in which homosexual acts have variously been accepted, tolerated, or prohibited. In looking at these cultures, however, we have to make a distinction between the sexual acts that take place between men and a gay lifestyle choice, which is a modern development. Ritual forms of homosexuality still exist among tribes in New Guinea – the Sambia, for example – and age-graded, same-sex relationships were accepted among several African peoples well into this century. However, in both these cases, once men became adults, they were expected to marry.

We have to await the development of the first urban civilizations and the invention of writing to find documentary evidence of early homosexual practices. The most ancient civilizations of the Near East give us few clues as to their attitudes to homosexuality, but the remains of an ancient Egyptian tomb shared by two court officials, Niankhkhanum and Khanumhotep, suggests that some form of gay life – even same-sex marriage – existed in pharaonic times, while in the warrior culture of ancient Assyria, men served the gods as same-sex temple prostitutes. The cultures of eastern Asia have a long tradition of tolerance for same-sex love. In Zhou Dynasty China (12th–3rd century BC), for example, age-graded relationships between men and boys were open and were celebrated in poetry.

DAWN OF MAN

Modern-day pre-industrial cultures, such as some of the tribes of New Guinea, preserve modes of sexual behavior that were common among our prehistoric ancestors.

Golden Greeks

In the West, the best documentary evidence for homosexuality during ancient times comes from the Greco-Roman period. For more than 1000 years, Classical Greek civilization and its heir, Imperial Rome, reigned supreme throughout Europe, the Near East, and North Africa. In its myths and legends, homosexuality appears side by side with heterosexuality. Zeus, the father of the gods, chose a beautiful youth, Ganymede, to be his cup-bearer and sexual companion, and Achilles, one of the greatest heroes of Homer's *Iliad*, famously mourned his lover, Patroclus, under the walls of

Troy. In classical history, one of the most famous figures of the ancient world, Alexander the Great (356–323 BC), married several wives and fathered children, and at the same time had a succession of male lovers.

Although many writers have characterized this period as a golden age of homosexuality, the Greeks themselves had no concept of a gay lifestyle, and no word in their language to describe such a choice. All Greek men were expected to marry and have children for the benefit of the city-state, but close male friendships sometimes developed into sexual relationships because there was no taboo associated with homosexuality. Age-graded, same-sex relationships were common, but were seen as temporary and lasting only until the boy matured into an adult male. However, there were limits to Greek tolerance, and men who were considered to have gone beyond the bounds of propriety were subject to public ridicule and sometimes much sterner sanctions, such as occurred in the case of the Athenian philosopher Socrates (469–399 BC), who was charged with "corrupting youth" and sentenced to commit suicide by drinking hemlock.

Latin lovers

The heirs and disseminators of Greek civilization, the Romans, had an ambiguous attitude toward homosexuality, which they called the "Greek vice." The early Romans were a puritanical, if not to say prudish, people, who frowned on all forms of material and sexual excess, until they themselves succumbed to it during the empire's decline and fall. Many leading Romans were known to have male lovers, most famously the Emperor Hadrian (AD 76–138), who made his lover Antinöus into a god, for whom temples were built all over the empire, after the young man's untimely death.

In the sophisticated cities of the vast and pluralistic Roman Empire, a strong

ANTIQUE PLEASURES

Many pagan civilizations of antiquity considered homosexual love to be a natural part of the human sexual experience. Although the Greco-Roman period is considered to be the "Golden Age" of homosexuality, these cultures had a far more complex and ambiguous view of homosexual conduct than some scholars would like us to believe. While accepted in myth, as in the love of Achilles and Patroclus (above), and in historical figures, such as Alexander the Great (left), all adult men were expected to marry and have children.

emphasis was placed on civic virtue, but this defined the Roman citizen's duties to the state and the emperor, and did not concern itself with private morality until the empire was Christianized in the 4th century by Constantine the Great (AD 285–337).

Into the darkness

Christianity is often blamed for the persecution of homosexuals that occurred in the West in the centuries following the collapse of the Roman Empire, but there is nothing in the original doctrine expounded by Jesus of Nazareth that rules against homosexuality. This comes from later, more intolerant periods of church history.

For centuries, the early Christians were themselves a misunderstood minority. Their belief in abstaining from all sexual activity, even within marriage, was considered at first ridiculous and later as subversive of the pagan establishment. However, it was the disappearance of urban culture after the collapse of the Western Roman Empire in the 5th century, more than the idol-smashing Christian zealots, that extinguished what little gay life there was in Europe. For many centuries, a rigid Christian morality persecuted homosexual acts as "one of the sins that cannot be forgiven." Paradoxically, homosexuality, in the form of homoerotic art, resurfaced in the very heart of the institution that condemned it – the Holy Roman Catholic Church. The leading religious artists of the Renaissance, Leonardo da Vinci (1452–1519) and Michelangelo Buonarroti (1475–1564), were both homosexuals. Michelangelo's homoerotic frescoes cover the walls and ceilings of the Vatican and his sculptures of muscular men adorn Italy's cities. Repressed and tortured, homosexuality triumphed in art, the one field in which it could exist.

Worlds apart

What Christianity had done in the Western world, Islam did for much of the East. The great pagan and Christian cities of the Levant disappeared under the assaults of desert tribesmen fired by the word of Mohammed or, like Constantinople, became isolated strongholds under strict martial and Christian law. During the Middle Ages, however, the cosmopolitan Islam of Spain and the Middle East was often far more tolerant of homosexuality than Christianity. The love of boys was celebrated in poetry and literature at the courts of the caliphs and of the Persian shahs.

As Western explorers traveled around the world, they came into contact with cultures with different attitudes to homosexuality in Asia, Africa, and, finally, the Americas. Not all the societies of pre-Columbian America were open to homosexuality. Among the Aztecs of Mexico it was punishable by death and, once conquered by the Spanish and Portuguese Catholics, they and the other conquered native peoples of the Americas followed the European lead in all matters sexual and moral. The story was repeated in the colonial scramble for Africa, where traditional cultures and sexualities were repressed by the Western powers. During these many centuries of persecution, only the cultures of the East and southeast Asia had a positive attitude to homosexuality. In Japan, Thailand, Korea, and China, male intimacy that transcended friendship and age-graded relationships were celebrated in art and legend. Again, there were restrictions: as with the Ancient Greeks, a gay lifestyle choice did not exist, and men were only allowed to engage in temporary same-sex relationships and only as long as they fulfilled their duties as husbands and fathers.

New dawn

For centuries, men and women in the Western world were forced to embrace conventional sexual morality and behavior, which only the rich and powerful could ignore. From the Middle Ages to the 20th century, there were many homosexual kings and statesmen, philosophers and artists, who were

BORN AGAIN

Michaelangelo's masterpiece, David, *exemplifies the homoeroticism found in the religious art of the Italian Renaissance.*

PIONEER SPIRIT

Magnus Hirschfeld was born in Kolberg, Prussia (now Kolobrzeg, Poland), in 1868. He published *Sappho und Sokrates* in 1896, in which he argued that homosexuality was a natural part of human sexuality, and that the laws against it should be abolished. He went on to found the world's first organization dedicated to ending the legal and social intolerance of homosexuals, the WHK (Wissenschaftlich- humanitäre Komitee, the Scientific-Humanitarian Committee), in Berlin in 1897. In 1899, the committee began the publication of the *Jahrbuch für sexuelle Zwischenstufen*, the first journal devoted to the study of all aspects of homosexual behavior. After collecting data from 10,000 men and women, he published his masterwork, *Die Homosexualität des Mannes und des Weibes (Homosexuality in Man and Woman)*, in 1914. In 1933, the Nazis closed the WHK and burned its library. Hirschfeld died in exile in France in 1935.

protected by their position or their genius. Change when it came was painfully slow. In the second half of the 19th century, the growing secularization of society, the emancipation of other minorities and women, and the new theories of human sexuality advocated by psychiatry began a slow process of change in society's attitudes to homosexuality.

The stirrings of reform came in Europe in the 1890s, when the German campaigner Magnus Hirschfeld founded the world's first organization dedicated to the study and decriminalization of homosexuality (see box, right). It is in this period that we first come across the word "homosexual," a term coined by Swedish campaigner Hans Benkert. At that time, in Berlin and Amsterdam, gay men began to emerge from the shadows to create the first visible gay culture, and by the mid-1930s, the word "gay" itself had acquired its modern meaning. These early voices were silenced by the Nazi holocaust and World War II, and it was only in the 1950s that they began to be heard again, in Holland, the UK, and the US. The world had been transformed by the war, and waited for gay men themselves to have the confidence to demand their rights. When the call for liberation came, it was not from closeted politicians or academics, but from a group of harassed men and women arrested in a small bar in New York's Greenwich Village, the Stonewall Inn.

WE ARE EVERYWHERE

Despite the dizzying pace of globalization that has taken place since the end of World War II, the world remains divided into distinct cultural zones, each with their own attitudes to homosexuality. As this book deals with the gay culture and lifestyles that have developed since 1969, it focuses on the Western world – North America, the European Union, Australia, and New Zealand, where Gay Liberation originated and has reached its most advanced stage, and on areas that share much of the same cultural heritage, the Russian Federation, Eastern Europe, and Latin America, where a gay lifestyle choice is becoming possible. However, while the Western concept of homosexuality is now being exported to the rest of the world, it is only one form among many. In other parts of the world, different concepts of homosexuality – some traditional and some new – stand as a testimony of the diversity that makes up the rainbow planet.

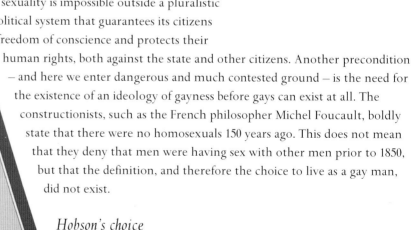

LEADING THE WAY

The ideology of gay liberation emerged in the pluralistic democracies of the developed world. (Chicago parade, 1999.)

FUCK HISTORY

French philosopher Michel Foucault (1926–84) expounded the constructionist case for the origins of homosexuality in his work on human sexuality.

Relatively gay

It is no accident that gay consciousness came into being in the West in the postwar period. In the light of the experiences of sexual minorities living under totalitarian and fundamentalist regimes, a lifestyle choice based on sexuality is impossible outside a pluralistic political system that guarantees its citizens freedom of conscience and protects their human rights, both against the state and other citizens. Another precondition – and here we enter dangerous and much contested ground – is the need for the existence of an ideology of gayness before gays can exist at all. The constructionists, such as the French philosopher Michel Foucault, boldly state that there were no homosexuals 150 years ago. This does not mean that they deny that men were having sex with other men prior to 1850, but that the definition, and therefore the choice to live as a gay man, did not exist.

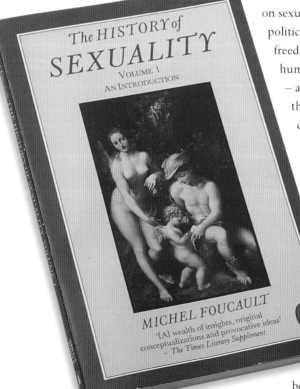

The HISTORY of SEXUALITY
VOLUME 1
AN INTRODUCTION

MICHEL FOUCAULT
'[A] wealth of insights, original conceptualizations and provocative ideas'
– *The Times Literary Supplement*

Hobson's choice

For many gay men and women who have felt impelled to come out in Europe and the United States in the decades following Stonewall, being gay or lesbian did not feel like a social construct or a choice, but an imperative that could not be denied. Many prefer to believe that there are two biological blueprints, which make some people straight and others gay. However, that notion, although comforting, conflicts with research on both non-Western and Western sexualities, such as the *Kinsey Report* of 1948,

MAN'S MAN

*For the past three decades, gay
men in the Western world have
been struggling to free themselves
from the stereotypes created
by the masculine/feminine,
gay/straight dualities inherent
in their culture.*

which found that most men fitted somewhere in between the all-gay or all-straight extremes (see page 53). However, Western culture is deeply imbued with Judeo-Christian dualism – the opposition of good and evil, male and female, and latterly, straight and gay. By defining so stringently what it is to be an ideal man in terms of gender and sexual preference, the culture also created its opposite: the un-masculine, non-heterosexual man. This dichotomy exists in its most extreme form in the cultures of southern Europe and Latin America, to which we owe the Spanish word *macho* (he-male). However, gay men in the developed world have firmly rejected all imposed stereotypes, and redefined both gender and sexuality to suit their own needs.

The Western experience

Both the word "homosexual" and the word "gay" were coined in Europe. The former, while it may sound ancient because of its Greek prefix *homo-*, meaning "the same," is just over a century old, while the latter, derived from the Old French *gai*, one of whose meanings is "addicted to pleasure," took on its current meaning in the teens of the 20th century. To these two words we must add a third, "queer," used by gay men since the 1980s, both as an act of social defiance and political self-definition. At the present time, it is only in the West that the words gay or queer can be applied to define a separate lifestyle, in which men and women make a conscious choice to seek emotional and sexual fulfillment in same-sex relationships, as well as base their economic and political choices on their sexual orientation.

CITY PAGEANT

Thirty years on, the city of New York hosts one of the world's largest and most colorful Gay Pride parades and street fairs.

Stonewall present: the United States and Canada

Each year, on the last Sunday in June, the area around the Stonewall Inn on Christopher Street is the setting for New York's Gay Pride street fair. The gay community has wrought a radical transformation in this city since that fateful day, June 28th, 1969. For a dozen blocks around, the streets, festive with rainbow balloons and flags, are crowded with men and women of all ages, genders, and ethnicities, celebrating their very own gay holiday season. Then comes the parade itself – starting at Central Park, continuing down Fifth Avenue, and ending at Washington Square Park – in which thousands march for three hours in a sultry East Coast sun, bringing together the most unusual bedfellows. The Radical Fairies, ASOs, and political activists ranging from Marxists to the Log Cabin Republicans, share the limelight with the mayor, the cast of off-Broadway shows, bands out for some free promotion, and the sweaty gyrations of the gogo boys on the dance-club floats. In the 1998 parade, the biggest cheer of the day was reserved for the gay and lesbian officers of the NYPD, marching proudly in uniform for the first time, and holding their first recruitment drive aimed at attracting more gays and lesbians into the police force.

Made in America The diversity of contemporary gay life in North America has been the subject of many books, the most famous of which is Edmund White's pre-HIV-AIDS tour of the US, *States of Desire* (1980). While homosexuality was decriminalized in Canada by the Trudeau government just before the Stonewall Riots in 1969, the legal position across the border remains confused and contradictory. Although the American gay community is the largest, wealthiest, most vocal, and best organized in the world,

even in 1999, 19 states still had "anti-sodomy" statutes, five of which were specifically targeted against homosexuals. The illegality of homosexual acts, however, has not prevented gay men and women from winning recognition of their rights in many areas of life, as we shall see in later chapters. To a foreigner, this situation seems absurd, until we remember that the US is not a single country subject to one national law, like a European state, but a federation of 50 states, each with its own laws, practices, and customs.

The life in Bryan The gay cultures of New York, Toronto, LA, San Francisco, and Chicago need little introduction here, but that is only one side of gay life in North America. In the 1990s, the real queering of the United States began when out gay men chose not to move to the big cities but to return to their home towns, large and small. In 1991, while I was visiting the small town of College Station, Texas, I had one night to sample the local nightlife. Checking through my *Spartacus Gay Guide*, I could find no listing for College Station itself, but one bar in the neighboring town of Bryan. Unlike the affluent, suburban university town of College Station, Bryan was poor and shabby, and at 10pm, deserted, except for a few suspicious-looking characters driving around in battered trucks. The outside of the bar was discretion itself: blacked-out windows with no sign. I pushed through the swing doors, stood in the doorway, and gawped. Couples were slow-dancing to a soulful ballad by Tammy Wynette. In the gloom it was hard to tell the sexes apart, as everyone was wearing jeans, check-shirts, and cowboy boots, but of the 10 or so couples, there seemed to be a 50/50 gay and lesbian split.

I marched up to the bar and sat down next to a good-looking young cowboy. His name (I kid you not) was Randy; he was 20, and he lived on a ranch two hours' drive from Bryan. When I told

QUEERING AMERICA

Gay men and women in the United States have now left the "gay ghettos" and live openly everywhere, from the major cities to the small-town "hicksvilles."

him that I was a French-born Englishman living in Tokyo, he looked at me as if I'd just told him I'd arrived from Mars. It became apparent that he had never made it further than Houston. I chatted to several other members of this little community: the barman, a lesbian couple, and more cowboys, who all seemed content with their lot and oblivious of the illegality of homosexual acts in their home state.

In and out of the Circuit Gay culture in North America has no shortage of detractors among the ranks of the religious and the New Right, but some of its most damning critics are gay men themselves. In *Life Outside* (1997), *Advocate* columnist Michaelangelo Signorile denounces the "Circuit mentality" that he sees as typifying fin-de-siècle American gay culture. The short-term pursuit of sexual pleasure fueled by orgiastic bouts of drug abuse and partying, he believes, not only imperils gay men's lives by encouraging them to have unsafe sex, but also ruins their chances of long-term happiness by preventing them from forming stable relationships. The excesses

CIRCUIT HIGHS

The White Party in Palm Springs, one of the established events on the Circuit calendar, attracts muscle boys and their admirers from all over the globe ...

INSIDERS

... but the Circuit's drug and sexual excess is under fire from within the gay community.

SPENDING THE PINK DOLLAR

If the 1970s were the decade of liberation and protest, and the 1980s of HIV-AIDS and the right-wing backlash, the 1990s were above all the decade of the gay man as consumer. Gay singles and, in particular, couples, shorn of parental responsibilities, have more disposable income than their heterosexual counterparts. However, while they remained economically excluded by legal persecution or their own left-wing ideologies, they could not be integrated into the mainstream economy. Businesses run by gays stepped in to fill the gap, but this did not go much beyond stores selling "gayola goods" – greetings cards, T-shirts, and novelty items – alongside fetish gear and pornography. One market that was particularly underserved was gay travel and, with the exceptions of bars and clubs, this is the sector that has shown the largest growth in the years since Stonewall (see Rainbow World, pages 112–157).

Signorile describes are not the preserve of gay men, but a feature of Western culture as a whole as it ditches the last constraints of conventional morality. In his horror at the uncertainty ahead, Signorile falls back on the safety of a gay version of heterosexual monogamy, itself a dying institution. Instead of looking back to an illusory ideal, however, perhaps we should be looking forward to the new forms of relationships that we will have to create in this new century to fulfill gay men's emotional and sexual needs.

Old world, new ways: Europe

If the 50 states of the US have trouble reconciling their differences, you would imagine that the countries of Europe – divided by centuries of bloody warfare, and without a shared language or culture to unite them – would find it even more difficult. However, in the aftermath of World War II, disunity was transformed into cooperation among the handful of countries of the European Economic Community. Now enlarged and with its own government and parliament, the European Union (EU) is poised to embrace the former countries of the Eastern bloc as its newest members.

While legislation and attitudes affecting gay men and women vary widely from the conservative Catholic and Greek Orthodox southern Europe to the Protestant and liberal

During the 1980s, it seemed that a parallel pink economy was developing, with its own retail, service, media, and financial sectors. While gay-owned and operated companies continue to cater for gay consumers, straight business has finally woken up to the potential of the gay market. This can be seen in the sponsorship of gay events by major corporations, such as airlines and drinks manufacturers, as well as the targeting of gay consumers by direct marketing and advertising.

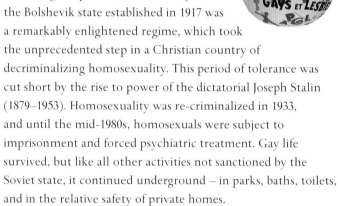

northern Europe, the existence of the supra-national EU has had a significant impact on the fight for gay rights. Enshrined in the European Convention on Human Rights is a clause banning discrimination on the grounds of sexual orientation. This has been used both to challenge discriminatory laws within the EU, and also to put pressure on prospective members, such as Cyprus and Romania (the only two European countries where homosexuality was still illegal at the end of the 20th century), to reform their own legislation. For millions of European gay men, life is good and getting better year by year. Not only have the discriminatory laws largely disappeared, and new laws granting equal rights in employment and partnership enacted, but, of greater importance, the battle to change hearts, as well as minds, has largely been won.

VIVE LA DIFFERENCE!

A hundred and fifty thousand celebrate diversity and Pride at Europride 1997 in Paris.

Out from the cold: Russia and Eastern Europe The "Evil Empire" of the Soviet Union and its satellite states has never had a good press, but in its first years, the Bolshevik state established in 1917 was a remarkably enlightened regime, which took the unprecedented step in a Christian country of decriminalizing homosexuality. This period of tolerance was cut short by the rise to power of the dictatorial Joseph Stalin (1879–1953). Homosexuality was re-criminalized in 1933, and until the mid-1980s, homosexuals were subject to imprisonment and forced psychiatric treatment. Gay life survived, but like all other activities not sanctioned by the Soviet state, it continued underground – in parks, baths, toilets, and in the relative safety of private homes.

The thaw began in the late 1980s, and in 1991 two organizations campaigning for gay rights in St Petersburg, Wings (St Petersburg Association for the Defense of Homosexuals) and the Tchaikovsky Foundation, were granted official recognition by the city. Finally, in June 1993, President Boris Yeltsin, bowing to pressure from the West, and in order to obtain a seat for Russia on the Council of Europe, finally decriminalized homosexuality. The main cities of the Russian Federation have small but growing scenes; the largest, naturally in Moscow, is sited around the Bolshoi Theater. Emerging from many years of silence and oppression, the Russian gay community has been quick to organize, and in 1996 it made its first proposal to the Duma, the Russian parliament, for a law on gay partnership.

Eastern renaissance Although the countries of Eastern Europe lived in the political shadow of their Russian neighbors for 50 years, they did not follow their lead in their social policies. Poland, which had legalized homosexuality in 1932, did not

re-criminalize it during the Communist era. Acceptance, however, has not come easily in this conservative Catholic country. The first attempt to create a gay and lesbian movement in Poland in the early 1980s was ruthlessly suppressed in 1985. Cowed but not defeated, the community began to publish its own magazine, *Filo*, in 1986, and in 1990, Poland's first gay rights group, the Lambda Association, was granted legal recognition. In June 1998, despite a city ban on a public event, Warsaw's gay community celebrated its first Gay Pride with the opening of a gay center and parties in bars and clubs. This pattern of early decriminalization coupled with the repression of any political organization is also found in other former Eastern bloc countries. Hungary, Czechoslovakia (now

PRAGUE SPRING

Liberation from Soviet rule in the 1990s allowed the new democracies of Eastern Europe to enact gay rights legislation, including anti-discrimination and gay partnership laws.

Real lives

GAY DOWN UNDER

Graeme Skinner – 39, single – is content to be at the bottom of the world, provided Sydney's weather and party calendar continue to deliver. He flats, works, and gyms in the heart of Sydney's "2010" gay ghetto, travels to Europe every three years, and is in daily internet contact with his Euro-trash friends. There have been three significant (and countless not-so-significant) men in his life, including a nine-year live-in relationship with a gay activist/academic, and a recent (predictably unsuccessful) attempt at long-distance love with a Dutchman. He himself is a freelance writer (about classical and early music), keeping him poor but contented, while his friends drive BMWs and wear Tag Heuers. Once a quiet studious adult, since his mid-30s he has self-diagnosed himself with DOA (delayed-onset adolescence), and now his CD shelves sag with Trance and Handbag. Perched somewhere between Lycra and leather, he's sure he's on the cusp of something (40?). However, seeking a lover of roughly his own age, he is chastened to remember just how many of his gay contemporaries did not make it to the millennium.

OPERA QUEENS

Sydney welcomes the world with open arms for its annual Lesbian and Gay Mardi Gras.

the Czech Republic and Slovakia), and East Germany decriminalized homosexuality in 1961, but their governments only tolerated their gay citizens as long as they remained silent and quiescent.

The end of Russian hegemony in Eastern Europe in the 1990s was immediately followed by the restoration of democracy and the emergence of gay life from the shadows. In the new united Germany, the former East Germans now have all the freedoms and rights of their West German neighbors. In Hungary, the Czech Republic, Slovakia, and Slovenia, government-backed legislation has established gay partnership and banned discrimination on the grounds of sexual orientation, bringing their laws into line with those of the most advanced Western European nations.

Queer Down Under: Australia and New Zealand

Along with the Republic of South Africa, Australia has some of the most advanced pro-gay rights legislation in the world. Until the 1980s, federal Australia suffered some of the problems of the United States, with different legislative regimes in force in each of its eight states. However, during the 1990s the country witnessed unprecedented progress in the areas of employment, anti-discrimination, and immigration rights nationwide. Sydney – the home of one of the world's largest gay Circuit parties, the Gay and Lesbian Mardi Gras (see pages 46–47) – and Melbourne have more in common with the urban gay cultures of London and Manhattan than the rugged outback, through which Priscilla and her sisters drove on their way to Alice Springs in *The Adventures of Priscilla, Queen of the Desert*, the first gay road movie.

It may come as a surprise to outsiders that New Zealand, a country with a city-sized population, a predominantly rural economy, and conservative Anglo-Saxon Christian antecedents, should be a model of enlightened pro-gay rights legislation. Whether this is as a result of the largely secular nature of Kiwi society, or the centuries of the pioneer tradition that it shares with its neighbor, this island nation at the ends of the earth has set an example for other countries to follow.

Mucho macho men: Latin America

In 1980, during a three-month stay while a student in Mexico City, I answered a newspaper advertisement for a cheap room in a shared house in one of the city's outlying districts. I arrived for my interview and was greeted by my prospective landlord, a Mexican man in his 40s, who introduced me to my four other housemates. It took me 30 seconds to discover that, quite by accident, I had landed in a gay household, and the next three months to work out what this actually meant in Mexico. The house was of traditional design, four rooms without doors leading onto a central courtyard. I shared a room fitted out with bunk beds with Pedro, a man of 26 who came from the rural state of Chiapas. He embodied the *machismo* of Latin America: straight-acting and direct, and quick to anger at any suggestion that he was "gay" or that he could have feelings for another man. At the opposite end of the spectrum was "Angela," a boy of 20 who dragged up to work in one of the gay bars in the city's gay district, the Zona Rosa.

Until the 1990s, when egalitarian relationships began to emerge among the educated middle-classes of Latin America's major urban centers, the division between active he-man and passive

SHEEP AND SLINGBACKS

It is no coincidence that it was Australia that gave us the world's first gay road movie, the wonderful Adventures of Priscilla, Queen of the Desert *(1994).*

INCA BABES

Sexual roles are often polarized in Latin cultures, opposing "macho" men to effeminate "maricón." (A drag club in Lima, Peru, 1995.)

effeminate *maricón*, which was a reflection of the distinct roles of men and women in Latin culture, formed the basis for same-sex interaction. In my household, this meant that Angela would occasionally get fucked by Pedro and the other straight-acting men, who would then deny categorically that they were gay.

Much has changed in Mexico and South America in the years since my first visit there. Democracy has returned to Chile, Argentina, and Brazil, signaling an end of government repression and police harassment of their gay communities, and allowing the emergence of commercial scenes and political organizations. Buenos Aires, one of the many thousands of Latin American cities to have passed anti-gay discrimination ordinances (1996), is now the home of South America's most active gay cultures.

Viva la Diva: Israel

To the consternation of ultra-Orthodox Jews, 2000 people marched through the streets of Tel-Aviv to demand equal rights for gays and lesbians at Israel's first national Gay Pride celebration in 1998. Loudspeakers blared out Israel's gay anthem, transsexual singer Dana International's *Viva la Diva*, which had just won the Eurovision Song Contest. In contrast, the Pride celebration in the conservative city of Jerusalem was held behind closed doors with an attendance of 200.

The Association of Gays, Lesbians, and Bisexuals in Israel was founded in 1975, but the movement could not develop until homosexuality was decriminalized in 1988. The greatest gains were made under the Labor administration of 1992–96, which enacted pro-gay and lesbian rights legislation in the areas of employment (1992) and access to the army (1993).

The Asian experience

For the centuries between the fall of the Western Roman Empire and the modern period, when homosexual acts were forbidden in the Western world, homosexual cultures flowered in the tolerant atmosphere of Buddhist southeast and East Asia. While this tolerance has remained in many parts of the region to this day, in others, under the influence of religious fundamentalism or Communist ideology, homosexuality has been repressed and forced underground.

In the bamboo closet: China

The Popular Republic of China (PRC) accounts for one-sixth of the world's population. If we apply the statistic that one in ten are homosexual, China should have

BROTHERLY LOVE

Freddy Gamarra is a 38-year-old graphic designer from Bogota, Colombia. He is the youngest of three gay brothers who all came out to their family in their teens. "It came as a shock to my mother," he recalls, "but she quickly accepted us. When we were younger, my brothers and I used to fight all the time, but after we came out, we became much closer and supported one another." His first gay experience was with a friend of his older brother when he was 15. He left home when he turned 18 after meeting Luís, a married man of 38 with three children. They stayed together for 14 years. "It's usual for young guys in Colombia to go for older men when they first come out, then when they get into their mid-20s, they find a partner their own age; and when they themselves get older, they close the circle by being attracted to younger men." Things have got a lot freer in the past 10 years in Colombia. "Young friends who are at university can be completely open about their sexuality. There are large gay communities in Bogota, Cali, and Medellín, and we have a great nightlife, but you still can't walk down the street hand in hand like you can in Europe or the US."

JEWISH PRIDE

Transgender singer Dana International caused controversy in Israel after winning the 1998 Eurovision Song Contest.

up to one hundred million gay men and women. Prior to the 1990s, however, this multitude was seldom seen or heard. Until the 20th century, China's traditional culture was tolerant of same-sex relationships between men, but the 1949 Maoist revolutionaries described homosexuality as a "moral degeneracy" imported from the West, and criminalized all homosexual acts. Since the end of the Cultural Revolution in 1980, police harassment and government repression has eased, and homosexuality has been discussed openly in the media. The 1990s were China's "coming out," though for most gays and lesbians this was in private to friends and family. In November 1992, an officially sanctioned event for gay men, called "Men's World," was held in Beijing. However, in 1993, following one of the sea-changes so characteristic of modern Chinese politics, all work in support of gay and lesbian rights or public education regarding homosexuality came to an end.

One nation, two systems China is not the monolithic entity it may appear to the Western outsider. This vast country not only contains huge cultural diversity, but also great social and economic variations. The deeply conservative rural areas are counterbalanced by the affluent cities of Shanghai and Guangzhou (Kwang-chou). There, a new middle-class has emerged, which is demanding greater economic freedom, and it is only a matter of time before this is translated into

CHINATOWN

Shanghai, southern China's premier industrial and commercial metropolis, is the home of a flourishing, but still largely hidden, gay culture.

RISING SONS

Economic giant Japan remains a deeply traditional Asian culture, with its own attitudes to homosexuality.

a call for greater personal freedom. The return of the former British colony of Hong Kong to China in 1997 aided this process. Under an agreement with the British, China promised to leave Hong Kong's social and political system unchanged for 50 years. While there was considerable uncertainty about the survival of the gay community after the Chinese takeover, these fears have so far proved groundless. Homosexuality was partially decriminalized in Hong Kong in 1991. There quickly emerged a small but vibrant Western-style bar and club scene, and political activists narrowly failed to introduce anti-discrimination legislation to Hong Kong's ruling council in 1993 and 1997. The first Chinese *Tongzhi* (a word covering gay, lesbian, bisexual, and transgendered people) conference was held in Hong Kong in 1996. Its delegates rejected the individualism and confrontational politics that characterized the Gay Liberation movement in the West, and decided that *Tongzhi* should be culture-specific and look back to Chinese homosexual cultures as models. The second *Tongzhi* conference of February 1998 welcomed 200 delegates from 17 countries, and established a foundation to fund projects in China and overseas Chinese communities.

Land of rising expectations: Japan

For all its economic power and technological sophistication, Japan remains a deeply traditional Asian culture. Lacking the West's concepts of sexual sin and guilt, Japan has never criminalized homosexual acts. Quite the contrary: it has idealized homosexual love as part of the relationship between master and pupil, lord and servant. However, the pressure to

A SALARYMAN'S LOT

Natsuo Matsuno, 33, is a "salaryman" working for the sales division of a major international publishing company in Tokyo. For the past four years, he has been sharing an apartment with his 40-year-old partner, Taku. Originally from a small town in western Japan, Natsuo prefers living in a big city "... where people don't care whether we're gay or straight, and we can be open about our relationship with our neighbors." Natsuo's passion is volleyball, which he has played since junior high. He is the captain of the team sponsored by the gay bar he frequents in Shinjuku, and Taku is one of his players. "There are many volleyball teams in Tokyo, both gay and straight, which compete in the same city league. As long as you like volleyball, sexuality is not a big deal." One of his fondest memories is of the beach volleyball tournament organized by one of the gay bars in Shinjuku in summer 1999. "We won all our games and became number one. The tournament was held on a public beach, and several drag queens turned up to entertain us with their 'gorgeous play'."

conform to heterosexual norms remains strong, and all Japanese, whatever their sexual orientation may be in private, are expected to marry. It was only in the 1980s, when several gay TV soaps and films made gay themes fashionable, that the idea of a separate gay lifestyle gained ground in the major Japanese cities.

Small is beautiful For the majority of Japanese men, gay life consists of occasional evenings in a bar, clandestine outdoor meetings, or visits to male prostitutes before they go home to their wives and families. A typical Japanese bar is intimate, with no more than a dozen stools at the bar and a couple of tables. It will only accept as many patrons as it can seat, and once you are inside, you are expected to spend the whole evening there, drinking, singing karaoke, and chatting to the "master" (owner) and the other patrons. The master is not just there to serve you drinks; he wants to make sure you will stay all evening and that you will come back. He finds out all about you,

TOKYO STORY

Gay life in Japan's cities is lived in thousands of small high-rise bars and love hotels.

LOVE UNTO DEATH

Every Japanese schoolboy knows the story of Lord Oda Nobunaga (1534–82) and Ranmaru, which is held out as a model of manly love and devotion to duty. One of the unifiers of Japan in the 16th century, Nobunaga was married with children, but the love of his life was his page, Ranmaru. Legend has it that when Nobunaga was about to be captured, the faithful Ranmaru assisted him in the ritual suicide of *hara-kiri*. The young man decapitated his lord, after Nobunaga had slit open his own stomach with a short sword. Then he set fire to the room and stood guard until the corpse was consumed by the flames, lest it be dishonored by his enemies.

INDIAN WINTER

Accounting for a sixth of the world's population, the Indian sub-continent remains closed to gay liberation because of religious and social conservatism.

JUST GOOD FRIENDS

While men can be seen openly walking hand in hand in most parts of India, the very mention of homosexuality is taboo.

entertains you, and will pair you off with a compatible fellow drinker. In short, he is barman, stand-up comic, counselor, and go-between all rolled into one. If you hit it off with someone in the bar, the master will suggest that you consummate the relationship in a nearby love hotel that rents rooms by the hour. Therefore, when a foreigner lumbers into a Japanese bar, expecting to cruise and pick up, he will neither feel nor be welcomed. However, this is not straightforward racism. He is not excluded because he is white, but because he cannot speak Japanese. Fortunately for the many expatriates and tourists in Tokyo and Osaka, a foreigner-friendly hybrid of the traditional Japanese and Western-style bar and dance clubs is becoming more common.

Passage to India: southern Asia

Hindu culture is not open to homosexuality, but it does have a place of sorts in its system of castes for men whose gender and sexual orientation do not fit the heterosexual model. The members of the hijra caste see themselves as a "third sex." Born male or hermaphrodite (although true hermaphrodites with both male and female genitalia are extremely rare), they must undergo castration to join the caste. Traditionally, the hijras were ascetic servants of the mother goddess who abstained from sex, but they now often work in the sex industry. India has no gay scene, and homosexual acts are illegal and severely repressed, but even in such hostile conditions, organizations lobbying for gay rights are beginning to emerge, such as the Humfasar Trust in Bombay.

The cultures of southeast Asia stand in marked contrast to those of the subcontinent. Thailand and the Philippines have never criminalized homosexuality, and same-sex relationships have always had an important place in their cultures, though the Western visitor is unlikely to experience any more than the commercialized versions of their homosexual cultures in the fleshpots of Manila and Bangkok (see pages 152–153). Although homosexual acts are illegal in Indonesia, homosexuality has always been an accepted part of traditional life. The irony of modern Indonesia's attitude to homosexuality is that it is among the new educated urban middle-classes that homophobia is beginning to emerge, while in the more conservative rural areas, married men openly have sexual relationships with other men.

The African experience

While many of the countries of Africa continue the repressive policies left them by their former colonial masters, one African country, the Republic of South Africa, is leading the world in its treatment of its gay and lesbian population.

SINGAPORE SLINGBACKS

Closed in the 1980s by Singapore's right-wing government of Premier Li, the TVTG bars and clubs are beginning to open for business once again.

BLACK IS BEAUTIFUL

South Africa is challenging the rest of Africa to follow its stand on gay rights. (Two Namibian men at Gay Pride, Cape Town, 1997.)

Boy wives: sub-Saharan Africa

Recent studies, such as *Boy Wives and Female Husbands: Studies of African Homosexualities*, edited by Stephen O Murray and Will Roscoe (1998), explode the myth that homosexuality was absent in pre-colonial Africa. However, these traditional homosexual cultures were repressed by centuries of colonialism and forced conversion to Christianity, and few survived into the modern period. One of those that did, that of the Azande of the southern Sudan, was studied earlier this century by British anthropologist E Evans-Pritchard. This warrior society allowed open sexual relationships between young men prior to marriage. However, this is a rare example, and in most countries, what the white man and the Cross began has been actively taken up by post-colonial regimes, many of which show little concern for the human rights of either their heterosexual or homosexual citizens. In this climate, homosexuality has been forced underground, and men must meet in private, buy sex from male prostitutes, or risk clandestine meetings in public spaces.

In a rare study of gay men in a modern African country, "Homosexuality in Dakar" (*Journal of Gay and Lesbian Studies*, 1996), Niels Teunis gives us an insight into the precarious lives of Senegalese men who meet in secret in a bar in the old city. With much of Africa afflicted by religious fundamentalism, dictatorship, poverty, and civil war, the outlook for gay men and women remains bleak. To add to this catalog of woes, the countries of sub-Saharan Africa are also the worst affected by the HIV-AIDS epidemic. Prejudice and discrimination prevent many sufferers from admitting their sexual preference, making preventative work to slow the epidemic even more difficult.

African rainbow: South Africa

Twenty thousand South Africans – white, black, Asian, and of mixed parentage – turned out to celebrate Pride 1999 in the streets of Cape Town, while 10,000 more danced the night away at the Johannesburg football stadium. A little over a decade earlier, when the country was ruled by a white minority government, it would have been unthinkable not only that the races should celebrate together, but also that they should celebrate their sexuality at all. Emancipation for the black majority in the 1990s coincided with a mass coming out for South Africa's gays and lesbians.

A MATTER OF HONOR

Iusif, a successful 28-year-old financial analyst, lives in exile in London. His family was forced to leave their native Iraq in the mid-1970s after Saddam Hussein came to power. He is out at work and with his non-Arab friends, and has an Irish boyfriend, but although he describes his family as "well-educated and extremely liberal," he cannot be open about his sexuality within his own community. "In the Arab honor system, a family's and a clan's standing depends on the behavior of its members. My mother once told me that she would rather kill her son than live with the shame of his being gay. My elder brother advised me to commit suicide!" Iusif dated girls until his 20s, and had his first sexual experience at the age of 24 with a man in his early 30s, who became a friend and role model. Saddened by the fact that he has to keep his sexuality a secret from his family and Arab friends, he sees it as a necessity. Nevertheless, he concludes, "I am proud to be an Arab, for the values my culture has taught me, and I am also proud to be sexually and politically gay."

ISLAND LIFE

Gay life in the West Indies is lived in the tourist areas or behind closed doors.

In recognition of the community's support of the anti-apartheid movement, the 1996 constitution drafted by the ANC government of Nelson Mandela was the first in the world to enshrine lesbian and gay rights. It can only be hoped that this example will encourage other African governments to embark on much-needed reform.

Children of Africa: the West Indies

Infamous for turning away gay cruise ships in the 1990s, the Bahamas is one of the post-colonial governments of the West Indies that still enforces the anti-gay legislation bequeathed them by their former European overlords. While clandestine homosexuality is common within the Afro-Caribbean community, the West Indian cult of manliness makes the acceptance of gay lifestyles an arduous challenge. Despite these difficulties, Jamaican gays have founded the Jamaica Forum of Lesbians, All-Sexuals & Gays (J-FLAG) to end discrimination and oppression, and campaign for the human rights of lesbians, all-sexuals, and gays on the island.

The Islamic experience

If you walk down the streets of Cairo, Istanbul, Baghdad, or Teheran, you will immediately notice two things: a scarcity of women, and physical intimacy between men. It is not just that their concept of personal space is smaller than that in the West, but also that men feel extremely at ease holding hands with each other and touching one another in ways that are not permitted between the sexes.

Forbidden pleasures: the lands of Allah

With few heterosexual outlets open to them, Muslims are not strangers to homosexual acts, but this should not be confused with the Western conception of homosexual identity. During the 1950s, when Western gays flocked to Casablanca, Tunis, and Marrakech to taste "forbidden pleasures," they were taking advantage of one of the paradoxes of North African male sexuality. The Islamic conception of manliness makes the Latin *macho* look like a sissy. A man is brave, honorable, upright, and strong in the faith, and he is always active. His masculinity is not put into question by his choice of partner — whether that be male or female — as long as he remains the penetrator. In these circumstances, if the recipient of his ardor is male, there can be no question of emotional involvement. A passive male is always considered to be dishonored and degenerate,

COLUMBIA PICTURES presents
THE SAM SPIEGEL-DAVID LEAN Production of "LAWRENCE OF ARABIA" A

Starring ALEC GUINNESS . ANTHONY QUINN . JACK HAWKINS . JOSE FERRER
ANTHONY QUAYLE . CLAUDE RAINS . ARTHUR KENNEDY
with OMAR SHARIF as 'Ali' and PETER O'TOOLE as 'Lawrence'

Directed by DAVID LEAN   Screenplay by ROBERT BOLT   Produced by SAM SPIEGEL   PANAVISION ®   A Horizon British Production in TECHNICOLOR ®

This copyright advertising material is leased and not sold and is the property of National Screen Service Ltd. and upon completion of the exhibition for which it has been leased it should be returned to National Screen Service Ltd.   Printed in England

with the exception of a boy, whose potential manliness is not compromised by being fucked by another man.

The proscription of homosexuality in traditional Sharia law makes a change in attitudes unlikely while the Islamic world is in the grip of religious fundamentalism. However, this has not always been the case. In the medieval period, Islam was often much more tolerant of homosexuality than Christianity. There is a rich tradition of homosexual poetry, such as the 8th-century court poet Abu Nuwas (see box, right), and an entire genre of Arabic literature devoted to the merits of male homosexual love. In the writings of the mystic Sufi sect, homosexual eroticism was a major metaphorical expression of the spiritual relationship between man and god, and medieval Persian fiction and poetry used same-sex relationships as examples of moral love. These examples of past toleration form the basis of the hopes of the exiled Arab men campaigning for gay rights in their home countries.

ARABIAN ADVENTURER

T E Lawrence ("Florence") of Arabia (1888–1935) is rumored to have had Arab lovers during his stay in Arabia in the early part of this century. (Peter O'Toole as "Florence" in the Oscar-winning 1962 movie Lawrence of Arabia.)

IN PRAISE OF WINE AND BOYS

Abu Nuwas (c760–815) is considered one of the leading poets of the Abbassid period (749–1258). He served at the court of the caliph of Baghdad, Harun al-Rashid (786–808). He appears as a character in the 15th-century collection of fantastical tales, *The Thousand and One Nights*. His poetry celebrated a very un-Muslim love of wine and boys. His poems have been anthologized in *O Tribe That Loves Boys: Nuwas Poetry*, edited by Hakim Bey (1999).

Equality

In the decades since Stonewall, gay men and women in the developed world have evolved from outcasts to full social and political citizens with rights and responsibilities. Now, in the 21st century, full equality is within our reach. This has been achieved not only in the face of political indifference and social prejudice, but also during the worst health emergency of modern times, the HIV-AIDS epidemic. Sadly, for the many gay men and women in the developing world, even the most basic right of existence remains a distant dream.

PRIDE

1960 1961 1962

In the round of Pride parades, marches, street fairs, and festivals that now take place across the globe, the circumstances surrounding the event that these celebrations commemorate – the Stonewall Riots – are often forgotten. This most celebrated moment in gay history is also the most misunderstood and misinterpreted.

Lighting the fuse: Stonewall

From the perspective of life in the 21st century, it is impossible to convey a real sense of what it was to be gay in the 1950s and early 1960s. In New York City, official harassment, raids, police entrapment, and discriminatory practices in the workplace, which left many gays open to blackmail, were the rule rather than the exception. By the late 1960s, however, things had already begun to change for the better. The evolution of attitudes toward homosexuality in society, combined with the pioneering work of the Mattachine Society of New York, led by activists like Dick Leitsch, had assured gay men and women's constitutional right to free association in "legal" gay bars, banned discrimination on the grounds of sexual orientation in city employment, and brought an end to police entrapment. Emancipation had gone further in other industrialized countries: in the UK, homosexuality had been partially decriminalized in 1967, Canada had followed suit in 1969, as well as several countries of the former Eastern bloc. With this background, why did Stonewall become the defining moment in the fight for gay rights?

The Stonewall paradox

It must be remembered that the 1960s was a period of extraordinary intellectual ferment and political rebellion throughout the world. Gay men and women, students, straight women, workers, and the ethnic minorities were demonstrating not just for their civil rights, but also for the respect that they had been denied for so many years. In 1969, mere toleration was no longer sufficient to meet the growing expectations of young American gay men and women. However, there is a paradox in the events of June 28th, 1969. The police raid on the Stonewall Inn, with which the birth of gay liberation will always be associated, was not primarily targeted against the gay community (though some still claim that it was), but to close down an illegal Mafia-operated drinking club that was breaking every health-and-safety regulation going.

In the beginning: the night of the raid

Imagine the scene: the early hours of a warm, moonlit morning in late June. The streets of New York's West Village are deserted. Most Friday-night revelers have gone home to their

BREACHBIRTH

The night the gay liberation movement was born, reconstructed for Nigel Finch and Rikki Beadle Blair's film Stonewall, 1996.

SHOCK TACTICS

In the 1970s, the mere sight of gay men and women walking hand in hand demanding their rights shocked and appalled the straight media and establishment.

7

1968

1969

OUT AND PROUD

In June 1970, one year after the Stonewall riots, thousands of gay men and women took to the streets of New York, LA, and San Francisco for the first Gay Pride demonstrations.

beds, apart from a few who are risking one last drink in one of the area's illegal after-hours drinking clubs. Shortly before 3am, a group of nine figures alight from their vehicles and gather in a huddle before heading off toward a known illegal drinking club, the Stonewall Inn, at 53 Christopher Street. A distant clock strikes the hour as Detective Seymour Pine leads his team of six men and two women plainclothed police officers into the bar. They quickly arrest the bar staff for serving alcohol without a license and order the customers to leave one by one.

The mixed crowd of men, women, and drag queens was relaxed and chatty – in a "festive" mood even, according to eye-witness accounts – as they waited for their friends to come out. No one present was surprised by the turn of events because this kind of raid was a regular occurrence in the Village. When the paddy wagons arrived, however, and the bar staff, three drag queens, and a lesbian customer were bundled inside, the mood of the crowd suddenly changed. There were catcalls and cries to topple the wagon. Bystanders started throwing coins and then bottles at the police to a chorus of "Pigs!" With the crowd closing in and the tables turned on them, Pine and his officers had no choice but to retreat into the bar and barricade themselves in. They were besieged until reinforcements arrived to disperse the crowd. The first "riot" had lasted 45 minutes.

The following day, the New York *Times* reported that 400 "youths" had been involved in a "mêlée" in Christopher Street, but the raid on Stonewall had started something. The following evening people gathered in the area once more, this time in their thousands. Shouts of

"Gay Power!" and "Liberate Christopher Street!" echoed around the streets of the Village. It was as if all of the pent-up frustration and anger that had built up over the years had found a focus. Barricades went up and protesters fought pitched battles with the riot police. The streets were not cleared until 3am. Disturbances continued sporadically for another three days. As the city counted the cost and cleaned up the mess, and the injured nursed their wounds, gay men and women had found their political voice and began to organize.

The aftermath: the politics of Pride

In political terms, the consequences of the Stonewall Riots on gay activists all over the globe were electrifying. In the US, gays flocked to join existing organizations, such as the Mattachine Society, which had branches in New York, LA, and San Francisco. Predominantly white and middle class, Mattachine had worked quietly and patiently for gay rights since the 1950s. Its aim was to win integration and acceptance for homosexuals, and it frowned on the politics of confrontation, preferring negotiation with the authorities, backed up by legal challenges to discriminatory policies when necessary. This softly-softly approach was at odds with the mood created by the riots. The newcomers were younger, more socially diverse, and espoused the left-wing ideologies and direct-action tactics employed by the more radical sections of the US civil rights movement.

Composed of such political and social diversity, the nascent gay rights movement quickly fragmented along ideological faultlines that have divided the movement to the present day: the centrist integrationists, who wanted to work within the established order to reform society, and the activists who called for freedom immediately and were not afraid to go onto the streets to fight for it. The latter founded their own group in 1969, the Gay Liberation Front (GLF). With some delay, the process was repeated in Western Europe, Canada, and Australia. While the GLF foundered in the US, other organizations took up the fight, including the GAA (Gay Activists Alliance, 1970), the Lambda Legal Defense and Education Fund (LLDEF, 1972; see box, page 39), the nationwide National Gay and Lesbian Task Force (NGLTF, 1973), and the Gay and Lesbian Defenders (GLAD, 1978).

FAMILY DIVIDED

The gay liberation movement appears united during Gay Pride marches, but since its foundation, it has been divided by deep ideological divisions. (Gay Pride, New York, 1998.)

HANDS ACROSS THE OCEAN

Inspired by activists in New York, gays all over the English-speaking world began to organize. By the early 1970s, Gay Pride demonstrations were taking place in the UK, Canada, and Australia.

Pride takes to the streets

Commemorations of the Stonewall Riots began the following year in the US with parades in four cities, including New York, where 2000 marched from the Village to Central Park, and LA, which saw 1200 march through Hollywood. In 1970 the act of publicly declaring one's homosexuality came as a tremendous shock to the straight establishment and media. They were going to have a lot more to deal with before the end of the decade. By 1974, LA was holding its first Pride festival in Hollywood along with its parade, setting a pattern of protest combined with celebration that has been reproduced worldwide. In New York, the 1970s saw up to 50,000 protesters take to the streets for the yearly march commemorating Stonewall.

LEGAL EAGLES

人 Founded in New York in 1972 as the Lambda Legal Defense and Education Fund, Lambda was the first organization in the world to establish itself to fight for lesbians and gay men in the courts and within the legal profession. Since its inception, Lambda has challenged the courts and constitutional system of the United States to win liberty and equal treatment for gay men and women, and people with HIV-AIDS. By making public the hitherto hidden lives of gay men and women, Lambda has won significant victories both in and out of the courtroom (on-line at www.lambdalegal.org).

VIVE LA PRIDE!

Although they started later than in the Anglo-Saxon world, Pride celebrations are now firmly established in continental Europe, boosted by the annual Europride, which is held in a different city each year. (Paris, Europride, 1997.)

Pride: a global crusade

For the first time in history, gay liberation had become a global crusade. Pride celebrations spread across the border to Canada, with Toronto's first Gay Pride Picnic in 1971. The first Pride marches in Australia and Western Europe began modestly in the early 1970s. London's first Gay Pride march was held on July 1st, 1972, under the auspices of the British GLF. Two thousand protesters marched along Oxford Street to Hyde Park and took part in other events including discos and a vigil outside the American embassy.

The themed Pride parades and marches of the 1970s called for action on specific gay rights issues, but except for a few cities with large, well-organized gay communities, Pride demonstrations failed to attract the participation of large numbers or to penetrate provincial centers. With governments worldwide taking measures to decriminalize homosexuality, or relaxing the enforcement of repressive legislation, and the gay liberation movement divided, most gay

PUT OUT MORE FLAGS

Exuberant displays, mass parades, riotous parties, and a carnival atmosphere are the hallmarks of Gay Pride celebrations around the developed world.

men were happy to enjoy the limited measure of freedom they had achieved. To the despair of activists, the 1970s were not the decade of mass political action but of mass hedonism, with a proliferation of bars, dance clubs, bathhouses, and backrooms, where gay men pushed back the limits of conventional morality and sexual behavior.

State of emergency: HIV-AIDS and the New Right

The HIV-AIDS epidemic of the early 1980s coincided with the rise of the New Right in the US and the UK. The dual threat galvanized the gay rights movement. On the one hand, it re-focused its energy on the issue of government inaction in the face of the HIV-AIDS crisis. This, and concerns raised by anti-gay moves by the Right to repeal anti-discrimination legislation in the US, were the prime movers that inspired the Second March on Washington for gay and lesbian rights (1987), which attracted a quarter of a million protesters to the federal capital to demonstrate for national legislation banning discrimination against gays and HIV-positive people.

In the face of the HIV-AIDS emergency, the gay community organized as never before. Beginning in the US with organizations such as Gay Men's Health Crisis in New York (1981, see page 70) and the San Francisco AIDS Foundation

GLOBAL ACTION

Founded in 1978, ILGA (International Gay and Lesbian Organization), headquartered in Brussels, Belgium, was the first worldwide association of organizations campaigning for gay rights. One of the most important aspects of ILGA's work is the lobbying of international bodies, such as the United Nations (UN), the Organization for Security and Cooperation in Europe (OSCE), the European Union (EU), and the Council of Europe, to which it was granted consultative status in 1998. ILGA was instrumental in the Council's decision to make the repeal of laws banning homosexuality a pre-condition for membership of the Council, putting pressure on prospective members, such as Lithuania, Romania, Albania, Moldova, and Macedonia, to repeal their discriminatory legislation. In 1997, ILGA played a significant role in ensuring that the Treaty of Amsterdam signed by the members of the EU includes a clause to combat discrimination based on sexual orientation.

The ILGA Our World conference takes place every two years and attracts delegates from all over the globe. ILGA has been supporting the emerging lesbian and gay movement and HIV-AIDS prevention in the former Eastern bloc countries since the 1980s, organizing annual regional conferences for the area from 1987 to 1996. The organization publishes *The ILGA Pink Book* (1985, 1988, and 1993), which highlights the legal, social, and political status of the international lesbian and gay movement, and includes country-by-country surveys describing the most recent information on the legal and social situation of lesbians and gay men (on-line at www.ilga.org).

(1982), new AIDS service organizations (ASOs) and pressure groups were established worldwide to support people with HIV-AIDS with direct-action programs, and to lobby national governments for funding. In 1987, playwright Larry Kramer helped to found ACTUP (AIDS Coalition to Unleash Power) in New York, and chapters were soon founded in all major US cities. The organization attracted young gay radicals who adopted confrontational tactics reminiscent of the early activism of the GLF in the 1970s to promote their cause.

From demonstration to celebration

Over 850 Pride events were listed in the world calendar for the year 2000. During the 1990s there was a dramatic increase not only in the number of countries celebrating the event – with fledgling events in South Africa, Israel, Japan, and the emerging democracies of Eastern Europe and Latin America – but Pride has also been disseminated to the provincial level within the US, Canada, and the countries of the European Union. The nature of Pride events has also changed beyond recognition. From the early political demonstrations by chanting, placard-waving activists, Prides have matured into week-long festivals of art, culture, and sports that attract major commercial sponsors and mobilize hundreds of thousands of participants.

Once ignored by the media and shunned by city and national governments, Pride events have now won the recognition of major world leaders. In 1991, Toronto city council bowed to the inevitable and officially proclaimed Pride Day for the first time, as 80,000 celebrated in the streets. Seven years later the city hosted MegaPride, with crowds estimated at one million, making it the largest celebration of its kind anywhere in the world. In Europe, the peripatetic Europride movement has held its yearly celebrations in France, Germany, Holland, Scandinavia, and Italy, consistently breaking local attendance records for Pride events.

MASS APPEAL

The double threat of the HIV-AIDS emergency and the emergence of the New Right mobilized gay men and women in the US as never before. A quarter of a million converged on the US capital for the Second March on Washington for gay and lesbian rights in 1993.

MR FRANK GOES TO WASHINGTON

Famously outed in the 1980s in a call-boy sex scandal, Democratic Congressman Barney Frank retained his seat in the United States Congress. He was elected to the Massachusetts State Legislature in 1972, where he served for eight years. During that time, he entered Harvard Law School in September 1974, graduating in 1977. In 1979 he became a member of the Massachusetts Bar. In 1980 Frank was elected to the United States House of Representatives, serving as a member of the Judiciary Committee and the Banking Financial Services Committee. In a recent evaluation of Congress, *The Almanac of American Politics* wrote: "Frank is one of the intellectual and political leaders of the Democratic Party in the House, political theorist and pit bull at the same time." In 1992, he published a book entitled *Speaking Frankly*, on the role of the Democratic Party in the 1990s.

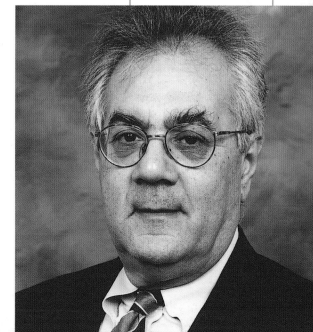

THE FREEDOM FLAG

The symbol of unity in diversity was first waved at San Francisco's 1978 Freedom Day parade. The original flag had eight colors: red, orange, yellow, green, turquoise, indigo, violet, and pink. Replica flags have six to eight stripes chosen from the following colors: red (life), orange (healing), yellow (sun), green (nature), blue (art), violet (spirit), indigo (harmony), and pink (sexuality).

THE PINK TRIANGLE

The pink triangle, or *Rosawinkel* in German, was sewn onto the clothes of homosexuals sent to concentration camps by the Nazis before and during World War II (1939–45). It was first used as a symbol of resistance and solidarity in the early 1970s. In 1975 it became the emblem of the Coalition of Conscience study group of the New York Civil Liberties Union. Starting in 1986, HIV-AIDS activists captioned the triangle with the words "Silence = Death." In 1987, the radical HIV-AIDS campaigning group ACTUP adopted the slogan, but inverted the triangle so that it pointed upward.

LAMBDA

The lower case of the 11th letter of the Greek alphabet was chosen as the symbol of gay liberation by the Gay Activist Alliance (GAA) of New York in 1970 after the Stonewall Riots. The letter is used in physics to designate kinetic potential. In 1974 lambda was adopted as the international symbol for lesbian and gay rights by the International Gay Rights Congress meeting in Edinburgh, Scotland.

The changing politics of Pride

Throughout the 1970s and 1980s, gay rights remained a cause espoused by the Socialist and Social-Democratic parties in Europe, Canada, and Australia, and the Democratic Party in the US, spearheaded by such groups as the National Stonewall Democratic Federation. The late 1990s, however, witnessed a significant shift of position among certain sections of the Right in the industrialized world. This began at the local level in the US for pragmatic reasons. In areas where the gay vote was important, conservative candidates standing for office had no choice but to support gay rights if they wanted to be elected. However, this was only a prelude to the "outing" of the Gay Right, with the emergence of such groups as the Log Cabin Republican Club, with 50 chapters nationwide.

The 1970s, 1980s, and 1990s witnessed the evolution of gay rights from the "pariah" cause of the 1960s into a civil-rights issue, subject to rational debate within the mainstream media and political parties in the 1990s. Admitting one's homosexuality is now no longer a bar to holding office at the federal, state, or municipal levels in the US. The situation for mainstream gay politicians is considerably easier in the countries of the European Union.

PINK POWER

The outing of a politician used to mean instant disgrace, but for UK cabinet ministers Nick Brown, Peter Mandelson, and Chris Smith (pictured here), admitting their homosexuality did not lead to a bar from political office.

ANOTHER BRICK IN THE WALL

With spokespersons such as actor Sir Ian McKellen, the London-based Stonewall group was founded in 1989 to lobby the British government for gay rights. Having successfully won the support of leading gay men and women from business, the media, and the mainstream political parties, Stonewall has mounted campaigns to equalize the British homosexual and heterosexual age of consent at 16, ban discrimination in the workplace, abolish the discriminatory legislation of Margaret Thatcher's Conservative government, and win immigration rights for same-sex partners.

LET IT ALL HANG OUT

London Pride has evolved from a political march into a city-wide cultural carnival, renamed London Gay, Lesbian, and Transgender Mardi Gras in 1999.

Sydney Gay and Lesbian Mardi Gras
Pride Down Under

Combining a three-hour parade through the center of Sydney, with floats ranging from whimsical and satirical to sexy and political, as well as the world's largest Circuit party, Mardi Gras embodies the new spirit of Pride. One hundred "marching boys" strut their stuff down the street five abreast, their modesty preserved by nothing more than the tightest of Lycra shorts and a very big smile. They stop to perform a synchronized dance routine as the crowd of spectators roars and wolf-whistles its approval. This is just one of the many memorable moments of the Mardi Gras parade, the largest festival in the Southern Hemisphere, which attracts a staggering 700,000 spectators to its closing parade, and 200,000 to a month-long schedule of events and parties celebrating gay and lesbian diversity in art, culture, and sport.

From riot to (r)evolution

In stark contrast, the first Mardi Gras, held on June 24th, 1978, to commemorate the ninth anniversary of the Stonewall Riots, attracted no more than 2000 participants. The day started badly when the police confiscated the truck with the PA system leading the parade. They moved in to break up the march an hour later, arresting 53 protesters. Further disturbances and arrests followed in the weeks after the parade. Many of the 104 arrested lost their jobs when their names were published in the local media. Despite this inauspicious start, the festival continued to grow. The first "official" Mardi Gras was held in 1985, with over 20 events and 30,000 spectators. The 20th anniversary celebrations in February 1998 saw the biggest parade ever, with 250 floats, as the culmination of a month-long festival that packed Sydney with visitors from all over the globe.

The morning after the morning after

The morning after is never a pretty sight, but at Mardi Gras, the morning after the morning after is the one that you'll want to avoid. Once the main party finishes on Sunday morning, clubbers drift toward the center of town, making impromptu stops to sunbathe in the alleyways between the show grounds and Oxford Street. They then make their way to one of the many "recovery" parties hosted by every club and bar in the city, where the fun continues until Monday morning.

Facts and Figures

700,000

watch the parade

17,000

take part in the parade

25,000

party the night away

EAST MEETS WEST

Representatives from every community, gender, and ethnic group take part in the Sydney Mardi Gras parade.

AND WHEN KYLIE CAME ON, THEY ALL WENT MAD...

As soon as the parade is over, 25,000 eager participants and spectators, clutching tickets they purchased six months in advance, converge on the giant halls of Sydney's Agricultural Show Grounds for the official Mardi Gras party. Despite the crush and queues, the atmosphere remains good-natured and friendly. Whatever your age, shape, or sex, this is your chance to dress up – paint yourself gold and wear nothing but a few interestingly placed sequins, drag up, or kit yourself out in full leather. On Mardi Gras night, you can be anyone or anything you want to be. Alcohol and substances flow freely from hand to hand, and the clubbers party on to live performances by the biggest local and international stars.

MARCHING ORDERS

Along with its famous opera house, the Mardi Gras marching boys are one of Sydney's most unforgettable sights.

Going for gold
Sports

The world of sport is one of the last heterosexist bastions to free itself from discrimination. Pressure from commercial sponsors and homophobia among media, fans, and sportsmen have ensured that very few leading gay and lesbian athletes have been willing to come out. There are notable exceptions, including tennis star Martina Navratilova and Olympic diver Greg Louganis, but there have also been tragedies, such as the case of British soccer player Justin Fashanu, who committed suicide in London in 1998 after a career marred by racist and homophobic prejudice.

Gay and lesbian athletes began to organize in the 1970s. Today, there are teams and clubs for every activity from aerobics to wrestling and every letter in between. Small local sporting festivals and leagues have since grown into international competitions rivaling the largest straight international sporting events. In Europe, the European Gay and Lesbian Sport Federation has held EuroGames since 1992, attracting up to 5000 competitors and many times that number of spectators to the games in Berlin (1996), Paris (1997), and Zurich (2000).

More than Olympian ideals: the Gay Games

In terms of gay sport, pride of place must go to the Gay Games, first held in the Kezar Stadium in San Francisco in 1982. The event, originally to be known as the Gay Olympic Games, but prevented from using the name by a court action, attracted a total of 1300 participants taking part in 16 sports. The 1986 games, also held in San Francisco, brought together over twice the number of competitors. In 1990, the games left the US for the first time and were held in Vancouver, Canada, attracting a growing number of spectators and competitors from around the globe. However, the breakthrough came with the 1994 Gay Games, held in New York City, which attracted an astounding 12,000 competitors and raised US$7 million in advertising revenue.

Going from strength to strength, the 1998 Gay Games held in Amsterdam took over the city for a week-long festival of sport and culture. Its 15,000 participants were more than matched by the 250,000-strong crowd that watched the spectacle of the opening parade on August 1st. Although the city had to bail out the event to the tune of US$2 million, it did not begrudge the money. In a statement, the mayor announced that he was proud that Amsterdam had been confirmed as the "gay capital" of Europe. The most popular event of the 1998 games, with 230 teams, was volleyball.

Among the outstanding competitors were veteran swimmer of the Munich Olympiad, Peter Prijdekker, who won five gold medals and set two new European Masters records in the 100- and 50-meter freestyle, and Daz Parker who took home her four medals, as well as her finalist's medal in the 50-meter freestyle. The games attracted coverage from the mainstream media. The first games of the 21st century take place in Sydney, Australia, in 2002.

The Gay Games

1982	*Gay Games I*	*San Francisco, US*
1986	*Gay Games II*	*San Francisco, US*
1990	*Gay Games III*	*Vancouver, Canada*
1994	*Gay Games IV*	*New York, US*
1998	*Gay Games V*	*Amsterdam, The Netherlands*
2002	*Gay Games VI*	*Sydney, Australia*

CAN'T RAIN ON OUR PARADE

Despite a ban on using the name "Gay Olympics," the Gay Games now rival in size and scope the largest international sporting events. (Gay Games, Amsterdam, 1998, above.)

GOING DUTCH

With 15,000 participants and 500,000 spectators, Amsterdam broke all records for a gay sporting event. (Switzerland's representatives at the opening parade, Amsterdam, 1998, right.)

FREEDOM

Few in 1969 would have imagined that a mere two decades after the Stonewall Riots, two men would marry in a ceremony recognized and sanctioned by their national government. The right to marry is one of many rights that gay men and women have campaigned for and won in the years since Stonewall, rights that cover every aspect of our daily lives – at home, at work, at play, and in between the sheets.

The fight for gay rights: one man's story

This is the story of Joe Stonewall, born in the early hours of the morning of June 28th, 1969. He's not a real person, of course, but through his imaginary birth and life, we can trace the evolution of gay rights from the time of the riots to the dawn of the new millennium. He would have been coming into the world when the Stonewallers were throwing bottles at the police in New York City – he was, of course, too young to notice, and his parents too busy with their new son to read the small item about a "*mêlée*" in the West Village in the New York *Times* the following day. The first question is: was little Joe born homosexual or did something make him "gay" at some point between birth and his first sexual encounter with a man? This is an important distinction with far-reaching political implications for gay rights, and as such is a subject that is still hotly debated worldwide.

Born not made: the genetics argument

The basis for the "essentialist" position is that homosexuality is a "natural" inherited trait, much like eye or skin color, through the presence of one or more "gay" genes. From the early 19th-century European Homophile movement to the late 1960s, pre-Stonewall gay rights campaigners often portrayed homosexuals as victims of a natural "abnormality," who, like other sufferers from other genetic disorders, should be pitied for a condition they could do nothing about rather than persecuted. Post-Stonewall, the portrayal of gay men and women as victims was forcefully rejected

NUCLEAR VALUES

In spite of many legal and social obstacles, an increasing number of gay men are raising their adoptive or natural children with their male partners.

by a new generation of activists, some of whom used the essentialist argument to claim that homosexuality was not only just as "natural" as heterosexuality but in many ways superior to it, as it embodied a more liberated expression of the human sexual potential.

While pro-equality campaigners who argue their case on the basis of genetic "difference" can claim with justice that to discriminate against homosexual people is as patently unfair as discriminating against people with black or brown skin, the sad truth is, however, that governments and people do discriminate on genetic grounds – even on imaginary ones, like the Nazi lunacies that triggered World War II. The latest advances in genetics, which have allowed scientists to identify and manipulate genes, have also raised the specter of screening the population for "undesirable" genes, and research to find "cures" for certain genetic "disorders." Despite this danger, the essentialist/genetics theory, as presented by Simon LeVay in *The Sexual Brain* (1993), can be used as a powerful argument to support full equality for gay men and women.

Made not born: the environmentalist case

Proof of their theories has so far eluded the pro-genetics camp. Apart from the rather obvious question of why a gene that discourages its own sexual reproduction could survive in the population, the theory also implies a black-and-white view of human gender and sexuality, with one genotype leading to the creation of exclusively "gay" humans, and another to their heterosexual counterparts. The ground-breaking *Kinsey Report* on male sexuality (1948) and later studies of human sexuality provide evidence that many men who consider themselves "gay" have had sexual encounters with women and many more who describe themselves as "straight" have had same-sex encounters at some point in their lives. The picture of human sexuality that emerges is that of a continuum with heterosexuality at one end and homosexuality at the other, with a lot of shades of sexual gray in between (see Kinsey Scale below), rather than a neat division between mutually exclusive opposites.

THE KINSEY SCALE

0	1	2	3	4	5	6
Exclusively heterosexual with no homosexual experience	Predominantly heterosexual, only incidentally homosexual	Predominantly heterosexual, but more than incidentally homosexual	Equally heterosexual and homosexual	Predominantly homosexual, but more than incidentally heterosexual	Predominantly homosexual, but incidentally heterosexual	Exclusively homosexual, with no heterosexual experience

A study of anthropology reveals that dualistic views of sexuality and gender are cultural constructs deeply ingrained in western Judeo-Christian culture, but not necessarily ones that are shared by all major world cultures. Although no culture has ever granted full equality to homosexual relationships, the cultures of pre-modern Japan, Native American Plain Indians, and pagan Greece and Rome regarded same-sex relationships as a natural part of the human experience.

To get back to little Joe Stonewall, if genes did play a part in determining his adult sexuality, then – according to the environmentalists – they did so in a complex interaction with his childhood environment and experiences. So what are the constructionist/environmental causes that might have given him a same-sex orientation? Theories abound, from Freud's "inversion" onward. Psychologists point to preconditions within the relationships within the nuclear family – absent or hostile fathers, dominant mothers, and so on – the permutations are endless.

The danger of the constructionist position is that it can be used to define homosexuality as a "sexual aberration" – an abnormality of psychological development that can be seen as "treatable." One of the most important steps forward in the fight for gay rights was the "de-medicalization" of homosexuality in the industrialized world. This was first achieved in the 1950s in Europe, in the Netherlands, and in the UK, where the government-sponsored *Wolfenden Report* (1957) recognized that homosexuality could no longer be

BREAKING THE MOLD

In 1948, Alfred Kinsey (1894–1956) shocked America with his groundbreaking study of male sexuality, which exploded the polarized distinctions between gay and straight men.

classed as a "mental illness." The American Psychiatric Association followed suit in 1973 after pressure from activists.

The bottom line is that there is as yet no single satisfactory theory to account for a process as diverse and complex as the development of human sexuality. There may be as many ways of becoming homosexual as there are homosexuals. Whether born or made, homosexual men and women in the developed world have finally won the right to exist, not only in the narrow legal sense because of the decriminalization of homosexual acts, but also as fully paid-up citizens, whose rights are respected by the vast majority of their peers.

The learning curve: Joe goes to school

Joe Stonewall goes to infant school and junior-high in the 1970s, missing out on the opportunity to emulate David Bowie's gender-bending antics. He hits puberty in the early 1980s and turns sweet 16 in the middle of the decade.

In many countries he can legally drive a car, leave school to work, marry a girl, and father a child, but in all but a few countries that have never criminalized homosexual acts, he will probably be breaking or "stretching" the law if he has sex with another man. This could be because all same-sex acts are illegal, as they still are in many developing countries, in two European states (Romania and Cyprus), and in 20 states of the "Land of the Free," the US. It could be because he has not reached the "Age of Consent" to have homosexual sex; or because certain acts, which are considered completely legal among heterosexuals, are still deemed illegal between two men. These legal absurdities notwithstanding, Joe, like many of his sexually mature teenage peers, is likely to taste "forbidden pleasures" with his friends, teachers, or acquaintances he has met in public spaces long before he reaches his country's legal age of consent.

The 1980s were not an easy decade for a gay adolescent. Although there were visible gay communities in all the major cities of the industrialized world, the HIV-AIDS epidemic was entering its most deadly phase in the West, hysteria and negative images abounded, and there were

LORDS OF DERISION

The passage of a law equalizing the age of consent for gay and straight people to 16 in the UK was delayed by the unelected right-wing House of Lords in 1999. However, the delay was short-lived, as the British government had accepted a ruling from the European Court of Human Rights that the different ages of consent contravened the European Convention on human rights.

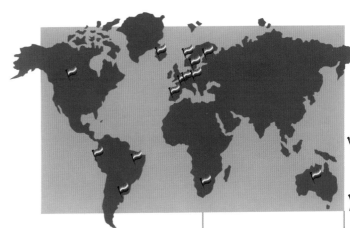

RIGHTS TO PROTECTION

Countries that provide protection from discrimination and vilification on the grounds of sexual orientation: Argentina *(cities of Buenos Aires and Rosario)*, Australia, Austria *(city of Bludenz)*, Brazil *(numerous states and cities)*, Canada, Denmark, Ecuador, Fiji, Finland, France, Iceland, Luxembourg, the Netherlands, New Zealand, Norway, Slovenia, South Africa, Spain, and Sweden.

Coming out is never easy, but teenagers in the developed world can now seek help from support groups and counseling services. (Still from Beautiful Thing, 1996.*)*

PROTECTION AT WORK

Countries that give protection against discrimination on the grounds of sexual orientation in the workplace: **Denmark, Finland, France, Ireland, Israel, Namibia, Slovenia, South Africa, and Sweden.**

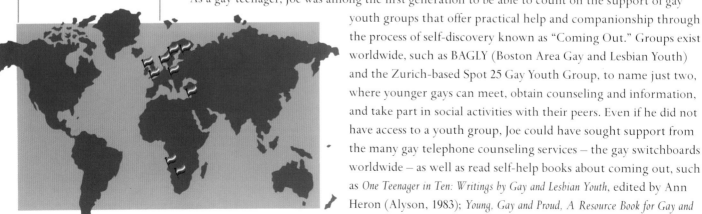

few positive role models with which a young gay man could identify. The disaster that was HIV-AIDS did nevertheless increase the level of awareness of gay people in the wider community. In Europe, at least, health education campaigns reached into every home and school with straight-talking leaflets and television campaigns that left little to the imagination. Fucking, oral sex, frottage, and condoms were all graphically described and explained. If young Joe Stonewall didn't already know that there were millions of other gay men in the world, by the late 1980s he did, and he also knew exactly what they did in bed.

Cracking open the closet door: Joe's "Coming Out"

As a gay teenager, Joe was among the first generation to be able to count on the support of gay youth groups that offer practical help and companionship through the process of self-discovery known as "Coming Out." Groups exist worldwide, such as BAGLY (Boston Area Gay and Lesbian Youth) and the Zurich-based Spot 25 Gay Youth Group, to name just two, where younger gays can meet, obtain counseling and information, and take part in social activities with their peers. Even if he did not have access to a youth group, Joe could have sought support from the many gay telephone counseling services – the gay switchboards worldwide – as well as read self-help books about coming out, such as *One Teenager in Ten: Writings by Gay and Lesbian Youth*, edited by Ann Heron (Alyson, 1983); *Young, Gay and Proud, A Resource Book for Gay and*

Lesbian Youth (Alyson, 1985); and *Beyond Acceptance: Parents of Lesbian and Gay Children Talk About Their Experiences* (McAllister, Wirth and Wirth, Prentice-Hall, 1986). In the developed world, Joe could also count on family support, because his parents would be much less likely than earlier generations to reject their gay son. They might even show their acceptance as many others have done, by joining groups such as the US-based PFLAG (Parents and Friends of Lesbians and Gays).

Out and about: Joe's rights to protection
Once Joe is "out," if he is a citizen of one of the countries listed (see box page 55), he can claim protection against discrimination and vilification on the grounds of sexual orientation. In addition, he can appeal against discriminatory national legislation. For example, he can appeal to the European court on the basis of the Amsterdam Treaty's ban on discrimination on sexual grounds and the European Convention on Human Rights, or to the International Court at the Hague.

9 to 5: Joe goes to work
It was only in the 1990s that real progress was made on the issue of protection in the workplace. While the situation in the US remains extremely complex, with legal challenges against discriminatory practices at the federal, state, and municipal level, the passage of a national law banning discrimination based on sexual orientation seems unlikely at the current time. However, if Joe Stonewall is born or resides in any of the countries listed (see box page 56), he can obtain protection from discrimination at work. To give just two examples of model legislation on this issue, in June 1996 the Danish Parliament passed Act 459 banning discrimination on the grounds of sexual orientation in the private labor market.

In 1995, President Nelson Mandela's government enacted South Africa's Labor Relations Act outlawing unfair workplace discrimination based on sexual orientation. One of the first employers

WORKING IT OUT
Protection from discrimination at work on the grounds of gender, race, or sexual orientation is one of the most basic human rights.

THE ARMED FORCES
Countries that allow gay men and women the right to serve in the armed forces: **Australia, Austria, the Bahamas, Belgium, Canada, Czech Republic, Denmark, Estonia, France, Ireland, Israel, Italy, the Netherlands, New Zealand, Norway, South Africa, Spain, Sweden, Switzerland, and the UK.**

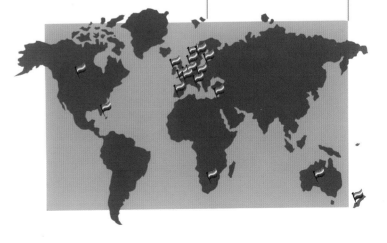

MEN IN ARMS

Thousands of gay men around the world have fought and died for their countries. Today, their right to be soldiers and openly gay is recognized by a growing number of national governments.

SEEKING ASYLUM

Countries where men and women can request asylum because of their sexual orientation: **Australia, Austria, Belgium, Canada, Denmark, Finland, France, Germany, Greece, Ireland, Latvia, the Netherlands, New Zealand, Norway, South Africa, Sweden, the UK, and the US.**

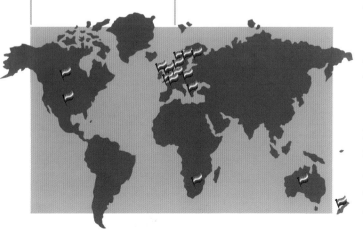

to endorse the ban in December 1995 was the South African Police Service, which issued new policy guidelines on gay and lesbian police officers. It noted that the police service recognized the right to equality in any appointment, promotion, or transfer, and that it "does not equate the ability, competence or potential of an individual in terms of their particular sexual orientation," adding that "no discrimination in terms of their sexual orientation shall be tolerated."

Fit for duty: Joe enlists

After President Clinton reneged on his election pledge to allow gays into the military, and a number of high-profile court cases in the 1990s, there can be few people unaware that Joe Stonewall will not be allowed to serve in the US Armed Forces if he is open about his sexuality. A similar ban in the UK was overturned in 1999. While court challenges are pending in the United States, other nations, starting with the Netherlands in 1974, allow homosexuals to join their armed forces, without the adverse effect on morale and discipline that other countries spuriously cite to uphold their bans. If Joe Stonewall were to join up in the Netherlands, for example, the law would permit him "to engage in consensual homosexual relationships, when off duty and away from military premises, both with a civilian or with a member of the armed services of the same or another rank."

Open door: Joe seeks asylum

If Joe Stonewall is unlucky enough to be born in a country where men and women are persecuted because of their sexuality, he can request asylum in any of the countries listed (see box, left) – although sexual orientation is not always stated as the main reason for granting the asylum request. In a landmark decision, and the first of its kind in the European Union in 1997, an Algerian citizen who had founded HIV-AIDS and human-rights organizations and, as a result, had been repeatedly harassed and assaulted by the Algerian police and Islamic extremists, was granted asylum in France on the grounds of his sexual orientation.

Trading places: Joe emigrates

Joe Stonewall has fallen in love, but if he and his partner are of different nationalities, how will he fare as far as immigration rights are concerned, either for himself or for his partner? If he or his partner are citizens of any of the countries listed (see box, right), he will have full or partial rights to apply for residence by virtue of their relationship. If Joe's partner is a Canadian citizen, for example, thanks to the efforts of LEGIT (Lesbian and Gay Immigration Task Force), as of March 1999, Joe has grounds to apply for immigration to Canada. Although the ruling falls short of giving full spouse rights, it states: "The separation of common-law or same-sex partners who reside together in a genuine conjugal relationship is grounds for humanitarian and compassionate consideration."

Here come the grooms: Joe gets hitched

Joe can "marry" his partner in a private ceremony anywhere in the world, as an ever-growing number of gay men and women have been

IMMIGRATION RIGHTS

Countries with immigration rights for same-sex partners: Australia, Belgium, Canada, Denmark, Finland, Iceland, Namibia, the Netherlands, New Zealand, Norway, South Africa, Sweden, and the UK.

WEDDING BELLES

A celebration of commitment or a parody of a failing heterosexual institution? The gay community remains split over gay marriage.

doing since the 1970s in a dizzying variety of settings, solemnized with even more diverse officiants, both civil and religious, including the worldwide Metropolitan Community Church (MCC). Unofficial gay marriages are common in the developed world, but have also been recorded in the developing world, in Cambodia, Colombia, Japan, Nepal, Taiwan, and Vietnam. Although gay marriage is not recognized in Japan, in January 1999, a 28-year-old musician and a 23-year-old office worker were the first to be joined in a traditional Shinto ceremony at the Wakamiya Hachimangu Kanayama shrine in Kawasaki. In a statement to the press, shrine priest Hirohiko Nakamura said: "At first I turned down their request because I was too busy to re-write the Shinto prayer for the ceremony. But their keen request moved my heart. I wish them good luck for their married life."

By the power vested in me ...

As soon as we leave the realm of private ceremonies, we enter the areas of legal obligation and financial benefits granted to partners. While full gay marriage has been outlawed with pre-emptive legislation in several US states, over 750 of America's leading private and public employers recognize the rights of the same-sex partners of their employees when granting leave and bereavement entitlements, and in some cases, health care and spouse benefits as well. The list of public bodies offering such benefits is headed by the United States Congress House of Representatives, which, since December 1995, gives the option to its members and their staff to register their same-sex partners as "significant others" for the purposes of House Rule 52, which prohibits them from accepting gifts from anyone besides family and friends.

The next level, which falls just short of full equality with heterosexual marriage, is the official recognition of a common-law or de-facto relationship. In 1989 Denmark became the first country in the world to introduce a law on registered partnership for same-sex couples. The registered partners have, with the exceptions of adoption rights and church weddings, the same rights and responsibilities as a heterosexual couple, including the provisions for divorce. The law is currently only valid in Denmark or in countries with similar legislation. The first couple to register was Eigil and Axel Axgil (1989). As of January 1997, 2083 couples, most of them men, had taken part in a simple city hall ceremony, of which 357 had later dissolved their unions. Similar legislation already exists in seven European countries, and is in the process of being enacted in several more, including

CROSS PURPOSES

Gay marriages are performed by both religious and lay officiants.

GETTING MARRIED

Countries where some form of same-sex partnership is recognized: Australia, Belgium, Brazil, Czech Republic, Denmark, Finland, France, Germany, Luxembourg, the Netherlands, New Zealand, Portugal, Slovenia, South Africa, Spain *(Catalonia)*, and Switzerland.

"I DO"

The Metropolitan Community Church solemnizes many as-yet-unrecognized gay marriages in the United States.

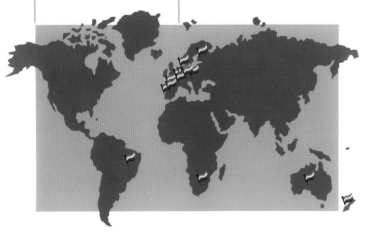

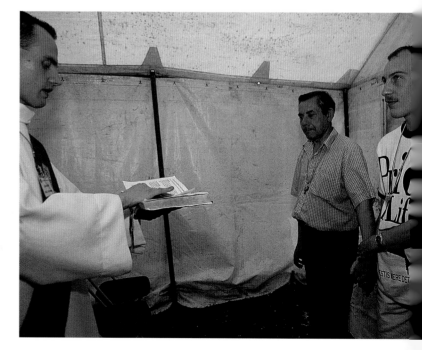

South Africa and France with the introduction of same-sex partnership as part of the Pacs (Pacte de Solidarité Civile) legislation of 1999.

Father Joe: adoption rights

One of the rights excluded from the registered partnership arrangements described in the previous section is adoption. If Joe wants a child but is not prepared to enter into a surrogacy agreement with a female partner, he can apply to adopt or foster a child in the countries listed (see box, right), although his male partner will not automatically be recognized as the second parent. In 1998, the Dutch government backed the granting of full adoption rights for same-sex couples for Dutch children. The measure is expected to become law in the early years of the new century.

HIS FATHERS' SON

In spite of midnight feeds and high college fees, many gay men are more than ready to embrace the joys and tribulations of family life.

ADOPTION

Countries where gay men and women are allowed to adopt children: **Australia (New South Wales), Belgium, Canada, the Netherlands, South Africa, the UK, and the US.**

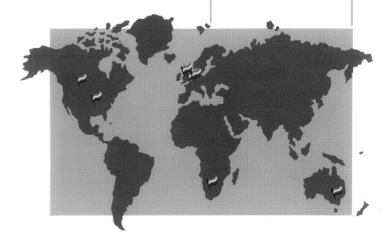

HOPE

For the fortunate in the industrialized world, HIV-AIDS is now a "manageable" condition. Awareness campaigns have slowed infection rates, while advances in drug therapies have done much to improve the quality of life for people with full-blown AIDS, and slow the progression of the disease in those testing HIV-positive. While there is a sense of hope in the countries of the developed world, the estimated 40 million living with HIV-AIDS in the countries of the developing world still await affordable drugs and a preventative vaccine.

We shall overcome: the war against HIV-AIDS

It may seem strange to include HIV-AIDS in the chapter dealing with gay rights, but from its very beginning the epidemic has been a human rights as much as a medical issue. Across the globe, it raised questions relating to homosexuality, drug use, prostitution, and promiscuity, which many governments were unwilling to tackle head on. The tragedy of the early years of the epidemic is that many deaths could have been avoided if health-education programs had been put into place as soon as the virus's method of transmission had been understood. The culprits were not only in the developing world, but most infamously among the leading industrialized nations, several of which were slow to take the measures necessary to deal with the epidemic.

SILENCE=DEATH

ACTUP's first largescale demonstration at the FDA Headquarters in Washington in June 1988 during the Ronald Reagan presidency.

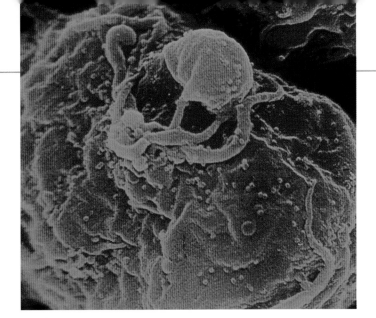

PREDATOR

The HIV virus infects a T-cell to produce millions of copies of itself, thereby fatally compromising the host's immune system.

The enemy within: HIV

Although a few still question the role of HIV (Human Immunodeficiency Virus) as the cause of AIDS (Acquired Immune Deficiency Syndrome), medical research and epidemiological studies have now confirmed its presence in the overwhelming majority of cases of the syndrome. Viruses are among the most primitive organisms on the planet – a simple collection of fats, proteins, and sugars – that cannot reproduce by themselves. They are parasitic entities that need the cells of other organisms to reproduce. Humanity has identified and learned to protect itself from many infectious agents, such as polio, smallpox, and TB, but HIV is a "retrovirus," which is distinct from other viruses because it contains the chemical Reverse Transcriptase that allows it to change its chemical makeup once it is inside a host cell. Constantly mutating, the virus is known to have several subtypes whose prevalence varies throughout the world: HIV subtype B is the most common strain in North America and Europe, while subtypes A, D, and E are most prevalent in the developing world.

Compared to airborne viruses such as influenza, HIV is not very infectious and is extremely fragile. It cannot survive outside the body, nor can it be transmitted through casual physical contact. To infect a new host, it must have a direct route into his or her bloodstream, most commonly in gay men through "unsafe" sexual practices (see box, right). Once in the blood, the virus seeks out the cells it needs to reproduce. The outer coating of HIV is equipped with protein receptors that allow it to attach itself to target cells. In the case of HIV, this is the T4 cell

KNOWLEDGE=LIFE

Unprecedented press, TV, and direct mailing companies brought the facts about HIV-AIDS into every home in the developed world.

HIV AND SEX

Since the coming of HIV-AIDS, there can be no sex involving physical contact with another man or woman that is 100 percent safe.

Very high risk
Fucking without a condom: "Barebacking" carries the highest risk for both partners because HIV is most prevalent in the blood, semen, and pre-cum of an HIV-positive person. A condom provides simple, effective protection.

Moderate to high risk
Unprotected oral sex: While opinions still vary as to the level of risk involved in sucking without a condom, there now exists a body of evidence that this is a risky practice for HIV-susceptible individuals and those with tears in the gums, mouth, and throat. A condom is recommended.

Unprotected fisting: HIV can be transmitted through tears in the anal wall and cuts from the fingers. Fisters should wear a lubricated rubber glove.

Low risk
Non-penetrative physical contact, kissing, mutual masturbation, and alternative sexual practices (eg, role play, toys, water sports, SM) that do not involve penetrative sex.

No risk
The only totally safe sex is remote sex (eg, telephone and cybersex), in which there is no direct contact between the partners.

DYING YEARS

Prior to the development of combination therapy, a PWA (person with AIDS) could only receive limited palliative care for opportunistic infections.

1982 PROGNOSIS FOR PERSON WITH FULL-BLOWN AIDS

Developed world: Fatal. Treatments available for secondary infections.

Developing world: Fatal. Very limited treatments available for secondary infections.

1985 PROGNOSIS FOR PERSON WITH FULL-BLOWN AIDS

Developed world: Fatal. Improved treatments for secondary infections.

Developing world: No change.

2000 PROGNOSIS FOR PERSON WITH HIV-AIDS

Developed world: "Manageable." Drug therapy is effective in most patients, restoring their quality of life.

Developing world: No change. It is hoped that health education campaigns will slow the epidemic in the 21st century.

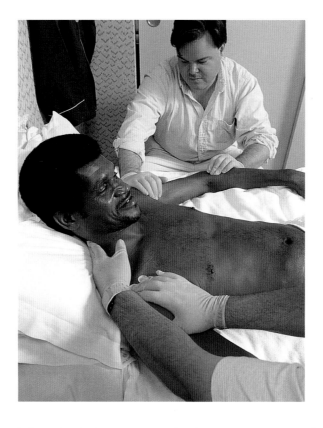

(also known as the CD4 or T-cell), which forms part of the human immune system. There are two kinds of T-cells: T4 and T8. T4 cells "switch on" the immune system when a disease agent is detected, causing T8 cells to destroy the infected cells and later to "switch off" the immune response. Once inside the T-cell, HIV injects its RNA and Reverse Transcriptase into the host cell's DNA and sets up a "factory" to produce more copies of itself. As the virus multiplies, it "buds off" or breaks out, leaving the T-cell damaged and unable to function.

With a failing immune system, the host becomes prey to a growing number of secondary infections, which, if untreated, lead to the host's death. HIV is unusual among viruses in that it kills such a high proportion of its hosts, and its strategy for survival depends on their ignorance of their infected status. After infection, new hosts will "sero-convert" or become HIV-positive, and the virus will be detectable in their blood with a standard HIV test. From this point on, although the hosts may not show symptoms of secondary infections for 10 years or more, they risk transmitting the disease if they do not take steps to protect their sexual partners.

The epidemic: the early years

HIV-AIDS is not a new disease. Researchers now know that it has always been present in Africa, where it was occasionally transmitted to humans through the hunting and eating of its original chimpanzee hosts. However, when the first cases of HIV-AIDS were reported in the US in 1979, doctors were mystified by a disease agent that seemed to target gay men by robbing them of their immunity to rare diseases such as Pneumocystis carinii pneumonia (PCP) and Kaposi's Sarcoma (KS). Due to the fact that the first patients were all gay men, doctors called the condition GRID (Gay Related Immune Disorder). In the next few years, cases were reported from countries around the globe. With no infectious agent identified, and the disease seemingly limited to homosexual men, right-wing groups and their associated media indulged in a shameful display of inhumanity, coining the term "gay plague," and worsened the epidemic by ignoring the growing body of medical evidence that heterosexuals were just as much at risk as homosexuals. In 1982, after cases of GRID had been reported among heterosexual men and women, drug users, members of African and Caribbean communities in the West, and hemophiliacs, the syndrome was renamed AIDS.

The epidemic: knowing the enemy

In 1983 Luc Montagnier of the Institut Pasteur in Paris isolated the LAV (lymphadenopathy-associated virus) as the cause of AIDS. A year later, in a move that created much discord between researchers and the governments of the countries involved, the US government counterclaimed that Dr Robert Gallo had isolated the HTLV-III retrovirus that caused the syndrome. The dispute was finally resolved in 1986 when an international committee decided that LAV and HTLV-III were the same virus, and ruled that both names should be dropped in favor of the new name: Human

Immunodeficiency Virus. Despite this success and a greater understanding of HIV's method of transmission, incorrect media reports in spring 1983 that it might be possible to become infected through casual household contact caused a worldwide panic.

During the first years of the epidemic, evidence was steadily growing that HIV-AIDS had become a global threat. The British Department of Health published the first official report on HIV-AIDS in the UK in 1983, announcing that three people had died. The first Australian death from AIDS was recorded in Melbourne in the same year. With the death toll mounting, a method of testing for the virus had to be found. In 1985 the US Food and Drug Administration (FDA) approved Robert Gallo's AIDS diagnostic kit based on the Western Blot test, which was later joined by the ELISA test. Testing and improved reporting methods were beginning to reveal the scale of the epidemic. By the mid-1980s, large numbers of people were known to be infected in Central Africa, where HIV-AIDS was called "slim disease," because of the wasting effect it caused in patients. In 1985, HIV-AIDS had been officially reported in 51 countries, but was suspected of being unreported in many more.

The epidemic: the fight back

By the mid-1980s it was clear that action was needed on a global scale. In 1986 the World Health Organisation (WHO) launched its global HIV-AIDS strategy, encouraging developing countries to admit that they had a serious problem. The first to do so was Uganda, where the Minister of Health declared that his country had a nationwide HIV-AIDS epidemic. Other African countries followed

RIOTOUS ASSEMBLY

Throughout the late 1980s and early 1990s, activists pressured national governments to obtain fairer treatment for people with HIV-AIDS (ACTUP, New York, 1989).

AIDS IN THE SPOTLIGHT

The HIV-AIDS epidemic has numbered many high-profile figures, both among its victims and its fighters. In very different ways, the tragic deaths of Hollywood actor Rock Hudson (1985) and British rock singer Freddie Mercury (1991) raised awareness of the disease. Actor Elizabeth Taylor, singer Sir Elton John, and the late Diana, Princess of Wales, are just a few of the many celebrities who have lent their names to the fight, working to promote HIV-AIDS awareness and to raise funds for research and primary care. HIV-AIDS has also had less fortunate meetings with the world of the media and advertising. In the late 1990s, Italian clothes manufacturer Benetton was forced to withdraw a world advertising campaign that showed a PWA (person with AIDS) in the advanced stages of the syndrome, after accusations that the company was exploiting victims of the epidemic for commercial gain.

suit, asking for WHO's assistance. The first nationwide health education campaign in Sub-Saharan Africa was launched by the Zambian Ministry of Health in 1986.

In the industrialized world, major awareness initiatives were funded, such as the British government's "Don't Die of Ignorance" campaign (1987), which delivered explicit leaflets to every household in the country. Also in the UK that year, Diana, Princess of Wales, opened the country's first specialist HIV-AIDS hospital ward. The fact that she did not wear gloves when shaking hands with patients was widely reported in the press and helped to change attitudes to people with AIDS. In 1987 the United States became the last major Western nation to launch a coordinated education campaign with the distribution of 107 million copies of "Understanding AIDS."

Shamed into action, governments began to take more practical measures to curb the spread of the epidemic. AIDS service organizations (ASOs) received the necessary recognition and funding, and needle exchange programs were established to prevent more drug users from becoming infected. Starting in 1987, a new class of antiretroviral substances came into use, holding out the hope that the progression of HIV-AIDS could be slowed. While the first of these, AZT (Retrovir), did not live up to its early promise, it led the way for a generation of new drugs. In the mid-1990s a growing list of drugs received approval from the FDA in the US, both for use singly or in combination, and a newly developed viral load test to measure the quantity of virus in the blood became a vital tool to provide information about the risk of disease progression.

In 1999, UNAIDS reported that the number of new HIV infections had declined in many countries due to safer sex practices, although worldwide the rate of infections continued to grow rapidly. Areas that reported a successful slowing of the epidemic included North America, Australia, New Zealand, Western Europe, and parts of Sub-Saharan Africa. The first HIV-AIDS hospice founded in San Francisco closed because fewer people were dying of HIV-AIDS in the US as a result of the success of new treatments. However, UNAIDS reports that the number of people currently living with HIV-AIDS in the world is 40 million.

The Lazarus effect: drug therapies

Prior to 1986, the only treatment available to patients who had progressed to full-blown AIDS was for the secondary infections caused by the syndrome. The discovery of AZT in 1986 offered the first hope that AIDS could be controlled if not cured. AZT was the first Nucleoside Analog Reverse

---

MAGIC BULLETS: HAART* DRUGS

Nucleoside Analog Reverse Transcriptase Inhibitors (NRTIs): AZT (Retrovir**), ddc (Hivid), ddI (Videx), d4T (Zerit), 3TC (Epivir), abacavir (Ziagen)

Non-nucleoside Analog Reverse Transcriptase Inhibitors (NNRTIs): delavirdine (Rescriptor), efavirenz (Sustiva), nevirapine (Viraumune)

Protease Inhibitors: indinavir (Crixivan), saquinavir soft gel (Fortovase), saquinavir hard gel (Invirase), ritonavir (Norvir), nelfinavir (Viracept)

* Highly Active Antiretroviral Therapy, see page 68

** Brand name given in brackets

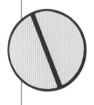

Transcriptase Inhibitor (NRTI) that interferes with the virus's reproductory process by targeting the chemical Reverse Transcriptase. However, HIV quickly demonstrated its ability to mutate and develop a resistance to the drug. In addition, AZT was highly toxic to the human body and caused debilitating side-effects in many patients. The real breakthrough came in 1995 when the Delta trial of combination therapy (later known as HAART – Highly Active Antiretroviral Therapy) showed that combining AZT with other drugs was much more effective than using AZT on its own. The success of this approach was confirmed by other trials, and dual combination therapy became the standard treatment.

Since it became widely available in the developed world in 1996, combination therapy has shown startling results by targeting different stages of HIV's life-cycle with three or more antiretroviral drugs (see box, page 67): two NTRIs and one protease inhibitor, or two NNTRIs and one NTRI. While new drugs, and improvements in dosages and resistance testing, have reduced the viral load of many patients to undetectable levels, researchers admit that they are just keeping one step ahead of HIV's ability to mutate and develop a resistance to the drugs used to fight it. Other approaches to combating HIV-AIDS include the development of therapeutic vaccines to restore limited immunity, and research into genetic immunity that has been identified in individuals who do not become infected, or those who are HIV-positive but are able to resist the progression of the disease for many years.

DAILY GRIND

A typical week's supply of antiretroviral drugs for combination therapy consists of 20 or more tablets, which have to be taken at set intervals, some with and others after food.

THE NAMES PROJECT AND AIDS QUILT

In 1987 a group of grieving friends, lovers, and relatives met in San Francisco to discuss the creation of a permanent memorial to the many who had died of HIV-AIDS, and to help educate others about the devastating effects of the syndrome. The original inspiration for the Names Project was an event after the San Francisco Candlelight March of 1985. One of the organizers, Cleve Jones, taped placards bearing the names of the more than 1000 people who had died of AIDS in the city to the walls of the Federal Building. The resulting patchwork reminded Jones of a quilt. Established in the Castro two years later, the Names Project was soon receiving donations and panels bearing the names of victims from cities nationwide. The AIDS Quilt, then consisting of 1920 3x6ft (1x2m) panels, was displayed for the first time during the National March on Washington for Lesbian and Gay Rights on October 11th, 1987. During its subsequent 20-city tour of the US, the total number of panels rose to 6000. As the century drew to a close, the Quilt commemorated some 41,000 people.

RED RIBBON DAY: WORLD AIDS DAY AND CAMPAIGN

The first World AIDS Day (WAD) was held on December 1st, 1988, as a day to remember those who have died of the epidemic, raise awareness, and send out a message of compassion, hope, and solidarity to those currently living with HIV-AIDS worldwide. In 1998, the World AIDS Campaign was launched to emphasize that AIDS was not just a cause for concern one day of each year. The Red Ribbon worn as a symbol of AIDS awareness was first shown on television at the New York Theater Tony Awards in 1991.

The Holy Grail: vaccines

While HIV-AIDS is now a "manageable" disease in the developed world, it remains a killer in those countries that cannot afford the available treatments. The only hope for the developing world is the discovery of a cheap, effective vaccine. There are currently two avenues of research in the development of HIV vaccines: preventative vaccines, similar to those used for infectious diseases such as polio, cholera, and tuberculosis, and therapeutic vaccines that can repair damage done to the immune system of an infected person. Among the latter group, Remune, which is made from whole-killed HIV whose surface has been stripped of a particular protein, is showing promise in human trials. Among the more conventional preventative vaccines that aim to prevent new infections by triggering immunity in an uninfected person (see box, page 68), several are in clinical human trials in Europe, the US, Southeast Asia, and Sub-Saharan Africa.

Life-savers: AIDS service organizations (ASOs)

In the early 1980s, with many national governments floundering and incapable of mounting a coherent policy to fight HIV-AIDS, the gay community took action. In 1981, the first ASO, Gay Men's Health Crisis (GMHC), was founded in New York City to provide HIV-AIDS care, education, and advocacy, followed a year later by the San Francisco AIDS Foundation and London's Terrence Higgins Trust. A model organization of its kind, in 1999 GMHC had more than 7500 clients, 6800 volunteers, and 206 staff. The breakdown of its budget of US$22 million was 67 percent from private donors and 33 percent from government. Its services include the provision of volunteer "buddies," legal assistance, counseling, recreational activities, education and publications, condom distribution, a telephone helpline, safe sex seminars and videos, and a weekly cable news show, *Living with AIDS*. Other organizations that have taken a much more confrontational political stand

on the HIV-AIDS issue include ACTUP (AIDS Coalition to Unleash Power; originally founded in New York by activists including playwright Larry Kramer, and now with chapters worldwide) and Peter Tatchell's Outrage in the UK.

Complementary Therapies

Research into psycho-immunology has highlighted the mind–body link's role in strengthening the immune response in those testing HIV-positive. Anecdotal evidence abounds as to the benefits of many complementary therapies, such as traditional Chinese medicine (TCM), homeopathy, and counseling, and prior to the development of HAART, many turned to these therapies, both as treatments for HIV-AIDS related infections and as boosters for their immune systems. Seattle's Bastyr University conducted the first trial of natural therapies with HIV-AIDS patients, HARP (Healing AIDS Research Project) in 1992. It concluded that several well-researched therapies slowed the progression of the disease without the side-effects of AZT, the only antiretroviral drug then available. Today, many HIV-positive people in the industrialized world are using complementary therapies in combination with HAART.

HEALING MIND

The power of the mind to heal the body and strengthen the immune response is harnessed by complementary therapies, such as meditation, traditional Chinese medicine, and homeopathy.

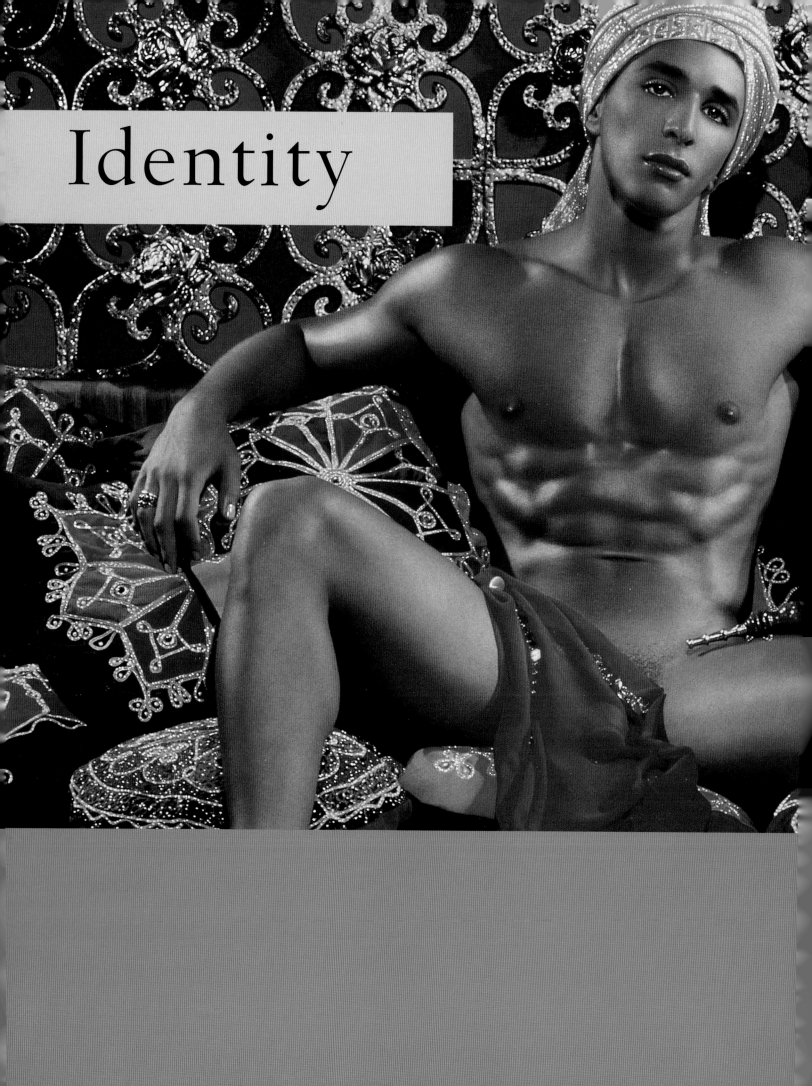

Identity

The decades of liberation heralded by the Stonewall Riots have brought undreamed of changes in both the private and public lives of gay men and women in the developed world. In private, we have reinvented our physical and sexual identities, and redefined our relationships; in public, we have given birth to a rainbow culture and a pink economy.

PHYSICS

Once stigmatized as weak and effeminate pseudo-males, gay men in the developed world have reinvented their physical identities. However, it is not only the gay body that has evolved over the past decades: gay men have often been the first to experiment openly with alternative sexualities (sometimes called fetishes) and new forms of relationships.

Sinners and perverts

Modern attitudes to homosexual sex in the developed world have their roots deep in Western culture's religious and medical past. Unlike the pagan cults of antiquity, pre-modern Christianity held a negative view of sex in general and homosexuality in particular. The church equated chastity with moral purity and salvation, and sex with the Fall of Adam and Eve and damnation. Sex was allowed within marriage to produce children, as long as neither partner enjoyed it. Homosexual acts, which could never be justified on the grounds of procreation, naturally fell under a severe interdict. As there was no concept of a separate homosexual "personality," which was only defined in the 19th century, any man who engaged in homosexual acts – or "sodomy or buggery," as these were called – was considered to have made a deliberate choice to take part in a sinful act against God. Although many Christian denominations have moved on to accept homosexuality, this remains the basic position of the Catholic Church and many fundamentalist Christian sects.

Even when the dead hand of religion lost its intellectual stranglehold on Western culture, its interdicts were subtly reinterpreted and taken up by medical science. Any sexuality that had been considered sinful because it deviated from the social norms of the day was now regarded as sexual perversion. At the dawn of psychiatry in the 19th century, this grouped homosexuality with such so-called sexual dysfunctions as masturbation, oral sex, and sex mania (wanting sex from more than one partner in your lifetime). The major shift in emphasis was that homosexuals were no longer seen as having chosen to commit "sinful" acts of their own free will, but were suffering from a mental illness that could be treated and possibly cured.

Old queens and grease-monkeys

Before Stonewall, many gay men had internalized one or more of these views of homosexuality: they saw themselves as sinners, mental cases, or criminals. Contemporary images of gay men were largely shaped by the high-profile court cases of the day. One of the most famous was that of the Irish playwright Oscar Wilde (1854–1900), who fell foul of the British laws against homosexuality in 1895. Wilde embodies one of the first Western stereotypes of gay men prevalent before Stonewall: the middle-aged, effeminate aesthete who is attracted to younger men – in other words, the "old queen" (though Oscar himself was happily married with children, and would never have identified with the image himself). The stereotypical old queen was a man haunted by self-loathing and sexual guilt, condemned to self-imposed celibacy through fear of legal pursuit and social disgrace. His sexual object was unattainable young, straight, "rough trade." While he was fastidious about his personal appearance, this did not extend beyond the surface of grooming and clothes. His body remained a hidden, shameful object that could not compare to the physiques of his sexual objects. The old queen is not dead – he lives all over the world, but he has been eclipsed by other images of gay men. He sometimes takes comic turns on our stages, and on movie and television screens, like the camp Mr Humphries in the hit 1970s British sitcom *Are You Being Served?*

STATELY HOMO

The late Quentin Crisp (above), an "old queen" of world renown.

SHRINKING SEX

19th-century psychologists such as Sigmund Freud (top) defined homosexuality as a mental illness.

However, that is only one side of the history of sex in the Western world before Stonewall. Evidence from court cases from the 19th century to the 1960s reveals the existence of a widespread homosexual sub-culture among the urban working-class and the lower ranks of the military, which only became visible when the straight establishment blundered into it by accident. Largely unknown to the general public, few, if any, of these men would have described themselves as homosexual, and certainly not as gay in the modern sense of the word. They were just doing what came naturally to men who had strong sexual drives and few heterosexual outlets. This pattern of homosexuality is still very much in existence in the Far East, Latin America, sub-Saharan Africa, and the Muslim world, where homosexual sex is commonplace but any form of gay consciousness is largely absent or repressed.

Steel magnolias

Another strand of pre-Stonewall homosexuality was transgenderism/transvestism. There is, however, an important distinction to be made between men who want to reassign their gender and live as women, and the many others, both straight and gay, who cross-dress occasionally for their own enjoyment or for professional reasons. Historically, female impersonation was seen as perfectly acceptable as long as it was for entertainment, as in the age-old and popular tradition of comic drag or of the Japanese kabuki *onnagata* (female impersonators). However, when

I'M NOT FREE

The antics of Mr Humphries in the hit 1970s British sitcom Are You Being Served? *did little to challenge established stereotypes of gay men.*

GIRLS! GIRLS! GIRLS!

Cross-dressing can be a lifestyle choice or just for fun. Two Muscle Marys show off their feminine side.

transgenderism/transvestism was associated with a life choice or with prostitution, it was repressed by the straight establishment.

Transgender/transvestite men have not had an easy time finding acceptance within the gay community either. Although they were prominent participants in the Stonewall Riots and the gay movements in the 1970s, they were quickly marginalized and then excluded by gay activists of all complexions because they did not correspond to the image of gay men that the activists wanted to promote. Although reassignment surgery is available in many countries, the legal recognition of gender change remains a contested issue.

Send in the clones

Stonewall transformed not only the straight world's conception of gay men but also gay men's image of themselves. The gay activists of the early Pride marches modeled themselves on the counter-culturists of the day, with long hair, beards, and slogan-plastered tie-dyed T-shirts. However, it was largely from outside their ranks – on the streets and in the bars of San Francisco – that there emerged a figure that was to define gay identity throughout the 1970s and beyond: the "clone." His uniform, which was self-consciously masculine – jeans, workboots, lumberjack shirts, and, of course, the ever-present mustache – empowered him by appropriating the outward symbols of straight blue-collar *machismo*. The clone identity functioned both as a signal to other gay men and as an act of defiance against the conventions of the day, which still obliged white, middle-class men to wear the regulation shirt and tie.

The 1970s was the decade of the "Permissive Society" in the industrialized world. This was reflected not only in the amount of sex taking place, but also in the type of sex that became acceptable. Liberated by the partial decriminalization of

VILLAGE VOICES

Clone camp with hit singing group The Village People, who gave us the classic "YMCA" and "In the Navy."

homosexuality and emboldened by the growing Gay Lib movement, Western men threw themselves into a non-stop orgy of sexual exploration. Bathhouses, saunas, and backrooms opened in the major cities to provide venues for instant sexual gratification, while hundreds of bars and dance clubs gave ample opportunities for cruising and casual pick-ups. The 1970s also saw the appearance of the first major gay sub-culture in Europe and North America – the leather scene.

The birth of the titocracy

While the majority of clones and leathermen were content with the outward trappings of masculinity, another group of gay men wanted to embody the masculine ideal as represented by the athlete or muscleman. Mirroring a trend for physical fitness that was taking off in the straight community, an increasing number of gay men joined gyms and started to work out. While a few opted for Jane Fonda's aerobics, most aspired to a cut-down version of the bronzed, smooth physique of the competitive bodybuilder. The ideal of the "Muscle Marys," as they became known in the 1980s, was well-developed arms, broad shoulders, large rounded pectorals with prominent nipples, a slim waist, and a "bubble butt." This hyper-masculine body, however, had many decidedly feminine attributes: it was spotlessly clean and perfectly groomed, and body hair was ruthlessly removed by shaving, waxing, or electrolysis. By the mid-1980s, every major gay neighborhood and resort had a gay gym, which quickly became one of the local community's social and sexual hubs.

A 1996 survey revealed that an astounding two-thirds of urban gay men in the US were working out, far outstripping the figure for straight men. The purpose of all this extraordinary effort is not success on the sports arena (though the mass participation in gay sporting events in recent years shows that this is now the motivation for an increasing number), nor health, as many Muscle Marys are not shy of using illegal and often dangerous anabolic steroids to achieve their goals. The real motivation is to win admittance to the sexual elite also jokingly referred to as the "titocracy" – the body-conscious aristocracy of the club scene that animates the party Circuit, and holds men such as porn star/escort Ken Ryker as their physical ideal. The original home of gym culture was in LA, New York, and Miami's South Beach; today, it has been exported worldwide, and you will find local versions of Muscle Marys training in gyms everywhere, from Brazil and Israel to Japan and Russia.

Into the woods

Although gym culture is now ubiquitous, it would be misleading to say that every gay man is a bronzed Adonis or aspires to become one. The reaction against Muscle Marys began in the 1980s with the emergence of "Bear" culture. The cult of hairy, overweight, bearded men emerged in the bars and clubs of San Francisco, where it is often associated with the leather/SM scene. "Beardom" has since been exported to Europe and beyond, often overlaying pre-existing sexual identities, as in Japan, where stocky, hairy, middle-aged men, who have always been admired as a sexual type in their own right, have adopted the name "Bear" to describe themselves as well as the North American Bear dress style.

Bootboys

Another identity favored by gay men that refuses to bow to Californian aesthetics is the skinhead, whose model originated in the working-class culture of the UK in the 1970s. The skinhead uniform of the 0-crop, tattoos, lace-up Doc Martins, jeans, and braces was first worn by members of Far-Right groups that espoused racist, homophobic ideologies. The gay man's adoption of the look of one of their oppressors is seen by some as disturbing and symptomatic of self-loathing. Another explanation is that gay men, following a well-established pattern, have empowered themselves by appropriating the outward symbols of a threatening identity.

Tribal ways

The most extreme rejection of conventional codes of dress and body decoration is to be found among the "new primitives." The main elements of this look are body-piercing and tattooing. Until the 1990s, the insertion of metal rings and studs into the body was a minority preference. Today, at least one piercing seems to be *de rigueur* for any self-respecting clubber. With the record for body piercings somewhere in the 100-plus range, devotees of metal body art are experimenting with ever more invasive procedures, such as the insertion of metal plates and studs under the skin to create visible ridges. Although many gay men consider tattoos to be little more than fashion accessories, others use them to signal sexual preferences, such as the tattooing of bands on the upper arms to indicate that the wearer is sexually active (left) or passive (right), or as identification with a particular sub-culture.

BEARING ALL

"Bear" culture emerged in San Francisco in the 1980s, in part as a reaction to the excesses of gay gym culture.

SKIN TO SKIN

Empowerment or self-loathing? Gay men adopt a look once sported by homophobic fascist "bootboys" in the UK in the 1970s.

DREAM BOYS

The Muscle Mary ideal has both hyper-masculine and feminine attributes (opposite page).

EROS

Sex is pleasure: a simple statement that even now makes the religious Right throw up its hands in horror. For centuries, both church and state have used the control of the sexual impulse to subjugate women and repress sexual minorities. The years of struggle for gay rights have also been a battle to free sex from social control. Gay men have rejected imposed norms to create new forms of sex. Just as homosexuality does not rule out heterosexuality, alternative sexualities (also known as fetishes) do not exclude one another as was once believed. Individuals can enjoy several types of sex simultaneously, or go from one to the other over time as their needs change.

NET GAINS

Meeting for casual sex has never been easier with the chat rooms and bulletin boards on the internet.

Getting it together

In the industrialized world, finding sex has never been easier. Men can indulge their sexual fantasies in indoor public venues, such as saunas and backrooms, as well as the more traditional parks and public toilets. The huge range of contact services now available through the printed media, the phone, and now the internet, offer undreamed-of opportunities to arrange encounters.

DOUBLE WHAMMY

Bad boy George Michael, who was caught with his trousers down in an LA "tearoom."

The great outdoors

Outdoor sex in parks or backstreets holds a particular fascination for many gay men. The combination of anonymity, danger of discovery, and endless possibilities acts as a powerful aphrodisiac. In countries with repressive legislation, public spaces are often the only venues for sex, but even in the industrialized world, where more comfortable and safer indoor venues are available, outdoor sex still retains its attractions. Every major city and gay resort has its cruising grounds or "meat rack" for sexual encounters during the day or night.

Tea for two

Another favored venue for gay sex is the public toilet, known in the UK as the "cottage," and in the US as the "tearoom." Police entrapment is still a common practice in the tearooms of the Western world, as British singer George Michael discovered to his cost when he was arrested in LA in 1998. Giving as good as he got, George produced a video to accompany the release of the song "Outside," which featured a glamorized version of the scene of his arrest. Paris had some of the most notorious tearooms in Europe, called *pissoirs*, which were mourned by the local gay community when most were torn down in the 1980s.

Intimate contacts

Advertising for sex started in newspapers as soon as the gay press made its appearance in the 1970s. Today's contact ads use convenient acronyms, abbreviations, and jargon to save on cost. For example, "XWEGWMWS top wltm GAM WS btm" translates as "Extra well-endowed gay white male water-sports top would like to meet gay Asian male water-sports bottom." Gay men have also found many uses for the humble telephone that Alexander Graham Bell could not have dreamed of: to place contact ads, to listen to pornography, and to cruise and pick up in multiple-user chat rooms. Phone sex, which is completely "safe," came into its own during the height of the HIV-AIDS epidemic.

Working it: prostitution

Prostitution – the oldest profession in the world – has never been a female preserve. Even during periods when homosexuality was savagely repressed in the West, there were always men ready and willing to turn to the trade, such as the sex workers in the Molly houses – the male brothels of 18th-century England. In countries where homosexuality is still illegal, prostitution is often one of the main types of same-sex interaction. Several non-Western cultures, including Japan and Thailand, have never criminalized their sex industries. In these countries, prostitutes enjoy a degree of protection from the harassment, abuse, and exploitation that their Western counterparts have had to endure.

While attitudes to homosexuality in the West started to change in the 1960s, it was not until the 1990s that sex workers began to benefit from increased tolerance for their profession. Even within the gay community, a known sex worker in the 1970s and 1980s was looked down upon. Although far from being accepted as a job like any other, prostitution is now practiced by a growing number of part-timers, who use it to finance their education or supplement their regular salary. Another trend is the development of a group of international male escorts-cum-porn stars who ply their trade in North America, Western Europe, and Australia, advertising in the local gay press as they move around the globe.

GAMEBOYS

As the stigma attached to prostitution decreases in the Western world, many gay men are taking up the "oldest profession" on a part-time basis to supplement their incomes. (Still from "sex-for-hire" movie My Own Private Idaho, 1991.)

The numbers game

As in the pre-Stonewall West, homosexual interaction in the developing world, which is often clandestine, anonymous, or limited to the sex industry, is not conducive to the establishment of permanent relationships. Liberation in the industrialized world has allowed men both to form stable, long-term sexual relationships, and to experiment with new forms of sexual interaction and alternative sexualities.

Monogamy is still an option for many gay men, though in the industrialized world, this is usually serial rather than life-long. Even when two men are in a one-to-one relationship, this can be closed – if they have agreed to be sexually faithful – or open – if they have a negotiated or have an implicit understanding that they are allowed to have sexual partners outside the relationship. Since the 1970s, open versus closed has been the subject of intense debate in the gay community. One camp claims that open relationships are a devalued form, entered into by men who do not have the necessary maturity to make a commitment to their partners. Their opponents argue that a closed relationship is an outmoded heterosexist institution, which does not correspond to the reality of human nature and limits a person's right to explore his full sexual potential. Many more fall somewhere in between these two extremes. Threesomes are a popular option with long-term couples who want to have outside partners but do not want a full open relationship. Although most of these do not go beyond three-in-a-bed sex play, they can occasionally develop into full three-way partnerships (know as troilism).

AS EASY AS 1, 2, 3

Although monogamy is still the preferred option for many gay men, "open" relationships and threesomes are now popular alternatives (opposite).

At the other extreme, many gay men have opted for promiscuity for part or the whole of their sexual careers. Men making this choice fulfill their emotional needs through close friendships, and their sexual needs with a succession of one-night stands or regular "fuck buddies."

Orgies or group sex became widespread in the 1970s with the opening of bathhouses, saunas, and sex clubs in the industrialized world but went into rapid decline during the 1980s HIV-AIDS epidemic. With the introduction of HIV testing and advances in treatment, group sex has regained its popularity, leading to fears among some commentators that this will trigger a second HIV-AIDS crisis.

Erogeny

The erotic stimulation of the male body is now almost an artform in its own right, with its high-priests of desire and its manuals, such as *The Gay Kama Sutra* by Colin Spencer (1996). Gay sex is not limited to the direct stimulation of the erogenous zones (mouth, nipples, penis, testicles, anus, armpits, and feet), but also explores the sexual aspects of bodily functions, role play, and fantasy.

Phallusies

Auto or mutual-masturbation, sucking, and fucking are the basic techniques used to stimulate the penis to ejaculation, but certain attributes of the organ are also sexual objects in their own right. A much-appreciated quality is size. The average male's erect penis of 6–6 ½in (15–16.5cm) does not satisfy "size queens," who yearn for the erectile impossibilities drawn by artists such as Tom of Finland, or the real outsized boys featured in *Inches* magazine.

Penis enlargement is now a major cash earner for cosmetic surgeons, but with gains of 1in (2.5cm) at most, surgical procedure is never likely to cure penis envy. Spectacular temporary enlargement can be achieved with a vacuum pump – a clear plastic tube that fits over the cock. Pumping out the air in the tube makes the penis swell to enormous proportions to fill the vacuum. However, the pump does not have any permanent enlarging effects, and over-enthusiastic users risk permanent damage, sometimes leading to impotence.

STAND AND DELIVER

*Anal intercourse, or "fucking,"
remains one of the defining sexual
acts between two gay men.*

In countries where boys are customarily circumcised as babies, the simple fact of having a foreskin, or being uncut, is seen as sexually exciting. Some cut men claim that an uncircumcised penis is more sensitive and are now reclaiming their foreskins through a lengthy procedure that involves stretching the remaining skin with weights until it covers the glans.

Backstrokes

Anal intercourse or fucking is the sexual practice most associated with gay men. Fucking with a condom is the recommended safer-sex practice to avoid HIV-AIDS transmission. "Barebacking," fucking without a condom, is by far the most unsafe practice. It should be avoided even when all present are HIV-positive, as it may lead to the transmission of drug-resistant strains of the virus. Other common ways to stimulate the anus is by licking (rimming), fingering, and using sex toys.

Fist fucking (also known as Red or FF) is thought to have become a common practice within the US SM community in the early 1970s. It is safe from the point of HIV or other STD infections, as long as the hand is protected by a rubber or plastic glove and the anal passage is liberally lubricated. Although small tears of the anal wall are unavoidable, as long the fistee is able to

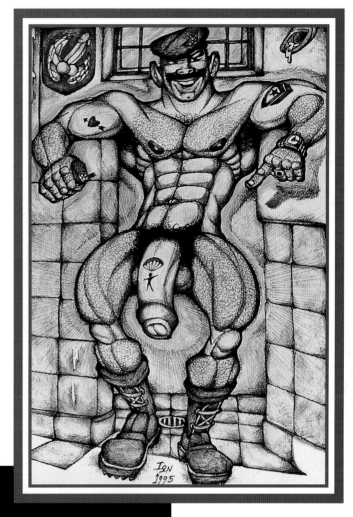

BIG

The cock, the focus of male sexual pleasure, can become an object of desire depending on its size and other attributes. (Paratrooper, by IΩN, 1994, above.)

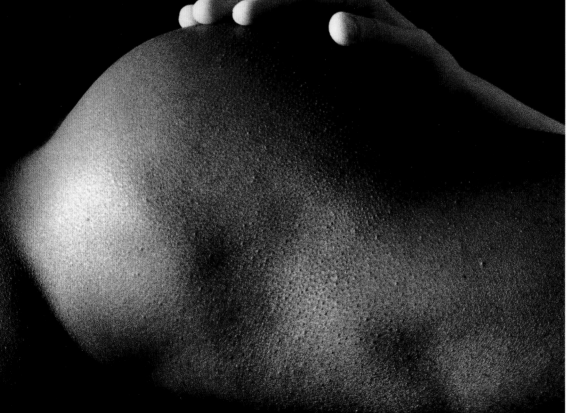

BUTT BLUES

Alternative anal play includes sex toys, such as dildos and butt-plugs, and fist fucking.

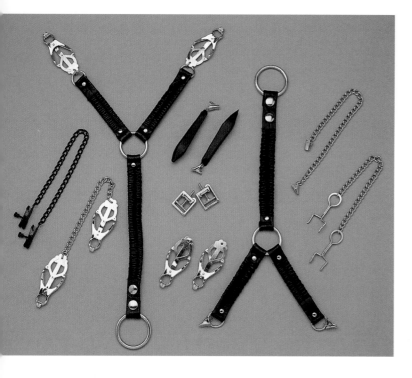

BIG SQUEEZE

For many, the male body's second most erogenous zone is the nipples, which can be stimulated with a range of toys and tit-clamps.

BREATHLESS

Strangulation can act as a powerful aphrodisiac, but safety considerations make it a dangerous game.

relax completely and the fister exercises due caution, there is unlikely to be any serious damage. Many gay men have anal douches or enemas before fucking and fisting for reasons of hygiene, but others also enjoy the procedure as a sexual act in its own right.

Titillation

The sexual lives of some gay men is focused on the nipples, which they will go to great lengths to enlarge and sensitize. Nipples can be stimulated by sucking, licking, biting, and pinching, but for the real aficionado of "tit torture" (TT), nothing short of nipple clamps with optional weights will do. One of the most common piercings is of the nipples. A nipple piercing can be used to indicate that the wearer is a top/active (left nipple) or a bottom/passive (right nipple).

All choked up

One of the reasons public hangings were said to be so popular in the Middle Ages was because the slow process of strangulation induces an erection and ejaculation in the victim. Although it is an extremely dangerous practice that has led to

many deaths, erotic strangulation or suffocation can be auto-stimulated with rope or plastic bags fitted over the head, or induced by a partner constricting the neck with the hands, arms, or a suitable object.

Definitely not vanilla

Once known as fetishes, alternative sexualities use an object (such as a sex toy), role play (such as SM), situation (such as outdoors), or activity (such as fisting), as the primary means to obtain sexual gratification. These preferences are by no means exclusive, and many gay men will experiment with one or more during their sexual careers. Alternative sexualities are now so widespread that the term "vanilla," which covers stroking, kissing, sucking, and fucking, is now used to describe sex that does not include an alternative element.

Sado-masochism The caricature of the SM "top" is a middle-aged man dressed in full leather and wielding a whip. While many on the SM scene do undoubtedly fit this stereotype, many more do not, being neither male, leather-clad, nor interested in physical suffering. In an SM relationship, both sadist, master, or top – the active partner – and the masochist, slave, or bottom – the passive partner – temporarily cease to be sexual subjects who can express their affection and free will, and consent to play the role of sexual objects in order to fulfill each other's fantasies. In essence, power provides the primary sexual

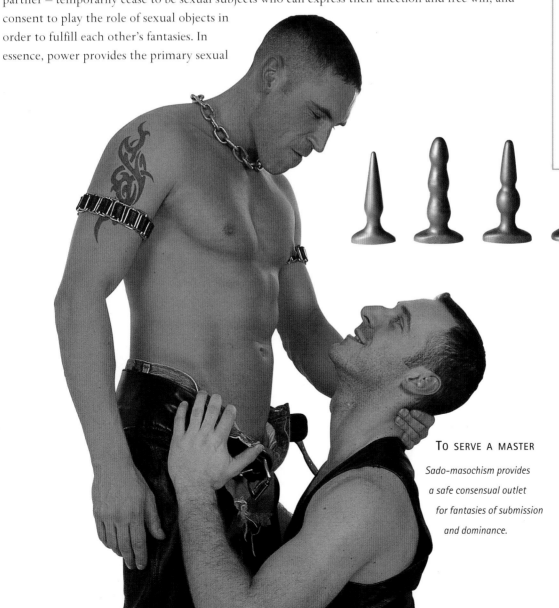
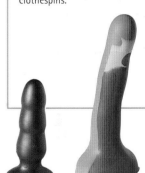

TO SERVE A MASTER

Sado-masochism provides a safe consensual outlet for fantasies of submission and dominance.

BOYS' TOYS

SM scenes are known for their use of elaborate equipment. Committed SMers have a fully equipped dungeon, complete with stocks, cage, sling, and a selection of restraints and sex toys. Top of the list among anal toys is any object that can be used to stimulate a pain/pleasure response. These range from specialist fetish gear such as dildos, vibrators, Ben Wa balls, butt-plugs, tit-clamps, parachutes, harnesses, hoods, gags, and cock and balls restraints, to more mundane objects found in the average home, such as snakebite kits and clothespins.

REBELS WITH A CAUSE

Modeling themselves on the street tough of the 1950s, as epitomized by Marlon Brando in The Wild One *(1954, pictured opposite), leathermen first adopted motorcycle jackets as their uniform. Today, leather – along with rubber and other associated paraphernalia – is much more than a look; it is a lifestyle with its own bars, clubs, organizations, events, and media.*

stimulus in the scene. For the top, the act of domination – be it ordering someone around, humiliating him, tying him up, or physically abusing him – is the expression of his desire to control his sexual object. For the bottom, the situation is reversed, and the sexual excitement comes from the sense of being dominated and controlled. How far either partner is willing to go is decided by negotiation before the scene begins, and either partner may interrupt the proceeding by using a safe word – a mutually agreed word that signals a time-out or stop. While this may appear to be a de-humanized form of sex, it fulfills deep-seated needs in both partners and provides a safe, consensual outlet for these desires. Taking part in SM sex does not rule out affection between partners once the scene is over, or indicate that the participants are unable to enjoy other forms of sexual behavior.

Bondage and discipline Bondage and discipline (BD) is often paired with SM to form the acronym BDSM. These two elements frequently feature strongly in dominance/submission role play. The bondage bottom can be restrained with rope, handcuffs, or leather cuffs, or completely encased in rubber, plastic wrap, or a body bag. The administration of discipline has its regional variants: North Americans with college fraternity antecedents favor "paddling" with flat wooden bats, the British prefer to use the standard public school punishment of "caning," while other nations make do with the hand, belt, or flogger.

Shaving Shaving is often used in SM role play, where one partner shaves the other, depriving him of one of the symbols of masculinity – his body and pubic hair.

All dressed up

Clothing plays a dual role in alternative sexualities. First, certain materials, such as leather and rubber, are chosen because of their feel or physical properties. Second, certain types of clothing enable the wearer to change his identity. Along with the leatherman (see below), other uniforms used in SM play include cops, firemen, soldiers – especially US Marines – sailors, jocks, construction workers, and cowboys.

CHAINS OF LOVE

*Bondage is the ultimate physical expression of the bottom's submission to the top.(*Slave, *by Kent, 1995.)*

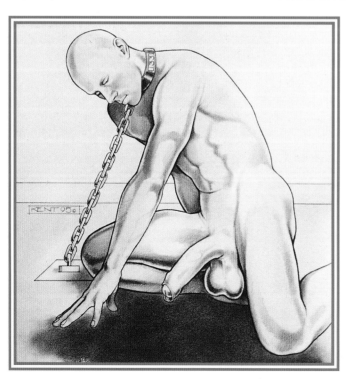

Leather The leather-clad street tough and biker of the 1950s, as exemplified by Marlon Brando in *The Wild One*, has always exerted a fascination for gay men. Like Tom of Finland's leatherman hero Kake, he is the ultimate incarnation of the *macho* fantasy – the social rebel and sexual outlaw. Gays in the United States and Europe adopted the leather look as early as the 1950s, but it was not until the 1970s that leathermen (more often than not without a motorbike) took to the streets in large numbers. In the years since, the leather community has developed its own ideologies, media, businesses, and organizations. Leather is an extremely broad church, encompassing men who wear it occasionally to go to leather bars and clubs, and men who wear it in daily life and aspire to live a full-time leatherman lifestyle. Sexually, the leather scene is similarly diverse. It would be as wrong to say that all leathermen are into SM as it would be to say that all devotees of SM are into leather. However, a certain degree of role play and domination/submission is taken for granted on the scene.

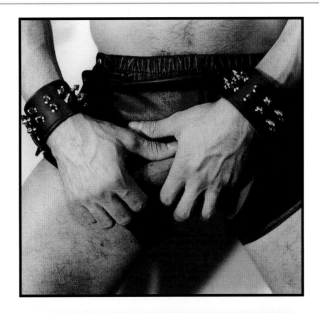

LEATHER KINGS

Although bars and clubs worldwide host wet jock, amateur strip, and best butt contests, the gay world has few international beauty pageants to rival Miss Universe or Miss World. There are some exceptions, and perhaps a little surprisingly, they hail from the leather scene: International Mr Drummer, held during the Folsom Street Fair in San Francisco during September, and International Mister Leather (IML), which attracts several thousand leatherfolk to Chicago at the end of May. While physical appearance does play a part in the latter event, it can by no means be described as a beauty pageant. Taking place over a long weekend, with a full schedule of parties, a market, and other leather events, IML culminates in the contest itself held on the Sunday. Some 50 contestants appear in a selection of leather outfits and are interviewed to gauge their suitability to hold the title. The final 20 contestants have to deliver a 90-second speech on the theme of leather in their lives. The winner walks off with a sash, a cash prize, leather goods, and the role of leather emissary for the year of his reign.

RUBBER STUFFERS

Increasingly used as a fashion statement, rubber first attracted gay men because of its sensual and constricting qualities.

Rubber Fashion gurus, such as French clothes designer Jean-Paul Gaultier, have introduced fetish wear to mainstream fashion. Items made of rubber, which would once have been hidden in the bottom of closets and worn only at home or in private members' clubs, are now paraded on the catwalk, and increasingly worn in dance clubs. Rubber owes its sexual attraction to its sensual feel and the constriction it imposes on the body. It is often combined with other forms of alternate sex play, such as SM and water sports.

Exhibitionism

Gay men enjoy both sides of the act of voyeurism – looking at sex, or being looked at while masturbating or having sex. At its most innocent, exhibitionism is the pleasure we feel when we are admired and desired. There are other forms of exhibitionism, such as the one described by the term flashing, which is more common among straight men who expose themselves to females in public. Exhibitionism can also have a domination/submission element, when the passive partner is exhibited in public to show the nature of the relationship.

Infantilism

Being treated as a child or infant is a sexual role that is seldom discussed in the gay community. Men who have this interest will acquire the paraphernalia of early childhood – clothes, diapers, bottles, and so on – and expect their partners to treat them as young children. This should not be confused with pedophilia. The physical and sexual abuse of children has become one of the most reviled crimes in modern times. In the late 1970s, pedophile organizations in the industrialized world (such as NAMBLA in the US) claimed that they were an oppressed sexual minority and campaigned for the abolition of the age of consent. This position was firmly rejected by gay activists on the grounds that gay sex between adults is consensual, whereas sex with children, who cannot give informed consent, is a form of sexual abuse and rape.

Water sports

Sexual play with urine, or "golden showers," can involve partners pissing over one another or drinking each other's piss. Urine is a sterile substance, and does not contain sufficient quantities of HIV to be infectious. It can, however, be the vehicle to transmit other sexually transmitted diseases.

Scat

The practice of sexual play using excrement, either by smearing or eating, is safe from the point of view of HIV transmission, but participants are at risk from hepatitis, which is transmitted through the feces of a carrier or infected person.

Wrestling

A popular sport with many gays in the industrialized world, wrestling has featured strongly at the Gay Games. Its attractions are twofold: the visual pleasure of watching two athletic males engaged in a contact sport very reminiscent of sex and, by taking part, the intense physical contact with another man, as well as the dominance/submission fantasies that can be played out on the mat.

FANTASY FIGHTS

Wrestling combines intense physical contact with submission/ domination role play.

PRIVATE DANCER

Many gay men find that the act of watching or being watched is a powerful aphrodisiac (right).

HANKY-PANKY

Colored handkerchiefs worn in the back pocket are a shorthand for sexual preferences, known as "flagging." Worn on the left, they indicate that the wearer plays the active role, and on the right, the passive role. Beware: the meanings of the minor colors can vary.

 Blowjobs
Light blue

 Fucking
Navy blue

 Fisting
Red

 Dildos
Light pink

 Titplay
Dark pink

 Water sports
Yellow

 Big dicks
Mustard

 Bears
Apricot

 Anything goes
Orange

 Shrimping
Coral

 Cowboys
Rust

 Spanking
Fuchsia

 Military
Olive drab

 Father/son
Hunter green

 Scat
Brown

 Hard SM
Black

 Bondage
Gray

 Rubber
Charcoal

 Jerking off
White

Shaving
Red/white stripe

In the eye of the beholder: pornography

Homoeroticism has always been a favored theme throughout the ages. It is found on ancient Greek vases, Roman mosaic floors, and Asian woodblock prints. Until the 1960s, gay porn was illegal in the developed world and had to masquerade as art, physical culture, or scientific research. Wilhelm von Gloeden's studies of naked Sicilian youths mark the beginning of artistic porn. Magazines depicting lightly clad athletes and musclemen were first published in the late 19th century in the United States, and titles such as *Physique Pictorial* continued to be published well into the postwar period. Another strand of pre-Stonewall pseudo-porn was the naturist magazine, such the British *Health and Efficiency*, which featured pictures of nude men and women in highly unerotic poses and settings.

Pressing the flesh

With liberation in the 1970s came an explosion of overtly gay porn magazines that abandoned the fictions of art or physical culture. Printed porn is now so common and widespread that it needs little introduction here, but there remain some interesting national quirks concerning what is permissible in print. In the UK, for example, although full-frontal nudity is allowed, erections above a certain angle are defined as obscene. Japan, which had no laws against pornography until the arrival of straight-laced Westerners in the late 19th century, has one of the most bizarre porn laws in the world. Whereas the acts and the intentions behind them are the prime concerns in Western anti-porn legislation, such as the US ban on images of fucking while the fuckee is tied up, the literal-minded Japanese merely forbade the showing of pubic hair and genitalia. The results can sometimes be rather startling. In many Japanese publications – including children's *manga* (comics) – the full range of straight and gay sex acts can be photographed and drawn, as long as the genitalia are not visible. This law led to the temporary banning of Madonna's *Sex*, because pubic hair was visible in the book.

In the 1990s, advances in computer-aided design and printing technology allowed the cheap production of glossy color magazines. No longer limited to major publications, such as *Euroboy*, *OG*,

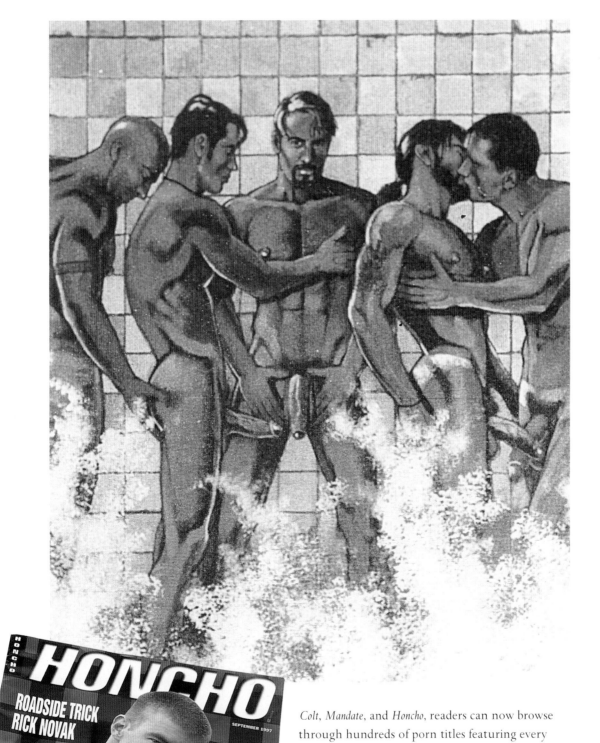

THE ART OF PLEASURE

Drawing and comic-book pornography is often used to depict fantasies that cannot be procured in other media. (Steam, by Kent, 1997, from the Tom of Finland Foundation's Erotic Art Gallery.)

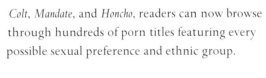

Colt, Mandate, and *Honcho,* readers can now browse through hundreds of porn titles featuring every possible sexual preference and ethnic group.

Comic relief

Although photography and video have replaced drawings and prints as the favored media for modern porn, homoerotic drawing and comic-book art still thrive, especially for the representation of fantasies that would be too difficult or expensive to recreate in other media. Japan's long tradition of erotic *shunga* prints continues in the *manga*-style comic strips of gay magazines such as *Barazoku, Sabu,* and *Adon*. European

PICTURE POST

The late 1970s and 1980s saw a boom in the publication of porn magazines worldwide. Shown here are Zipper (UK), OG (Australia), and Honcho (US).

LOOK BACK IN ANGER

Critic Kenneth Anger, author of
Hollywood Babylon, *was a pioneer
of underground gay porn in the
pre-Stonewall US.*

artists have produced erotic works in the adult-oriented *bandes desinnée* (graphic novel) format, first made popular in France and Belgium, while American artists have been inspired by the DC and Marvel comic-book style to produce short illustrated stories. US-based Leyland Publications has issued the work of many of the world's leading gay comic-book artists, including Oliver Frey, The Hun, Etienne, and Stephen, in its *Meatmen* series. The undoubted master of the genre, who has spawned many imitators but never been equaled, was the Finnish artist Tom of Finland (see box, page 103), whose work is preserved and published by the Tom of Finland Foundation.

A star is porn

Film was coopted to make porn soon after the Lumière brothers patented their Cinematograph in 1895. Made under repressive censorship, the gay porn films of the pre-Stonewall era were often tediously slow, with a few, heavily edited sex scenes. In any case, the patrons of sex-movie theaters were more interested in other members of the audience than the films on the screen. Although there was a brief vogue for home movies on cine film, it was the advent of home VCR technology in the 1970s that revolutionized both the medium of gay visual porn and the habits of its viewers. For the first time, men could choose from a large selection of inexpensive videos to watch at home, available by mail order or from the growing network of sex shops.

Until the 1980s, American porn videos dominated, with their bronzed, muscular Adonises mouthing a few clipped lines, before getting down to the business of sucking and fucking in stage sets with all the interest and style of American daytime soap interiors. In the 1990s, the Europeans came back strongly with their own products. These were sometimes much better plotted, such as the works of the French director Jean-Daniel Cadinot; set in more exotic locations, as in the Brazilian fantasies of Kristen Bjorn; or featured a different aesthetic of the male, as in the films of Bel Ami showcasing East European youth. As with the print media, the availability of cheap video cameras and now digital cameras has led to an explosion of videos featuring alternative sexualities, as well as a growing market in home-made amateur porn.

Surfer porn

According to a 1997 survey, an astounding 58 percent of internet traffic that year was porn-related. Anyone who has surfed the web knows that by typing the word "gay" into a search engine, you will hit literally thousands of sites, most of them commercial porn sites. These consist primarily of text stories, galleries of photos and erotic drawings, and, increasingly, of video feeds. The latest trend is for interactive live shows, in which "performers" chat and comply with the wishes of viewers, exploiting the web's fast-expanding video-conferencing capabilities. Commercial sites charge for access privileges on a daily, weekly, and monthly basis. A large number of non-commercial sites also feature free porn, but these are usually protected by age-verification gateways, such as Adultcheck™ and Mancheck™, which charge a yearly fee for the use of their services. The web is also famous for its weird and wonderful sites, and devotees of the truly bizarre and alternative should find plenty of free amateur sites. Just type in the magic word in the search engine ... but be careful what you wish for.

the prime of the Athletic Model's Guild

PREVIOUSLY RELEASED AS VIDEO

HOME MOVIES

The advent of cheap VCR technology in the 1970s revolutionized the gay porn industry.

Only connect
The Internet

If E M Forster had written his famous plea, "only connect," today, he would probably be advised to get a better modem. The internet's superb text and graphics capabilities are fast replacing telephone chat lines as the preferred means to enjoy remote sex. However, this is only the dawn of the internet age; as computer memory expands and modems get faster, full digital audio and video-conferencing will take over from text-based and still-image-based services.

Selling yourself on the net
To encourage visitors, many commercial and non-commercial web sites offer contact-ad services, where you can post pictures of yourself, a brief profile, and an e-mail address for replies. Another way to advertise is by publishing your own home page, where you can include text, your own gallery of images, links, video feeds, and sound clips. Commercial and private special-interest sites are often linked to one another in "web rings," such as the Leather Ring or the Escort Ring.

On-line cruising
For the present, the most popular way to cruise the net is by joining live text-based chat rooms, which can be accessed either directly with web browsers, such as Netscape or Internet Explorer, or through the Internet Relay Chat (IRC) network. A typical browser-based chat room is gay.com (http://www.gay.com), which offers over 700 rooms on three cyber "floors." The rooms are divided by geographical location, such as "East Coast Men" and "UK Men," or preferences, such as "The Gym," "College Guys," and "Leather." To access the worldwide IRC chat room network, you will need to download software such as IRCLE or MIRC.

One of the boys (censored) bares all on a live Cuseeme video connection with a QuickCam.

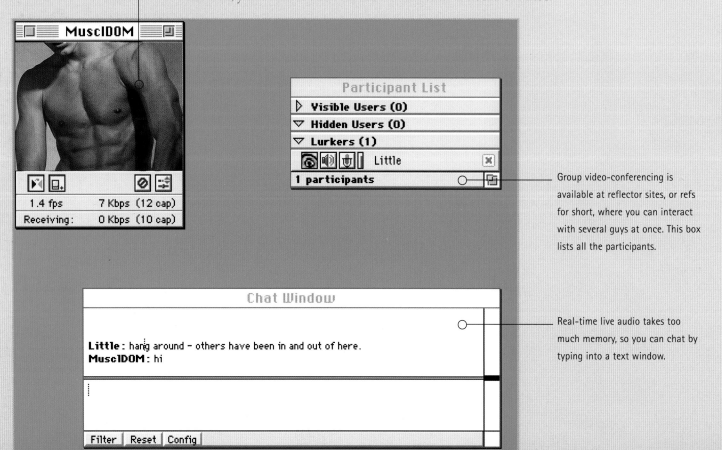

Group video-conferencing is available at reflector sites, or refs for short, where you can interact with several guys at once. This box lists all the participants.

Real-time live audio takes too much memory, so you can chat by typing into a text window.

On the #gaymuscle channel on the IRC network are 348 men, who are regulars and can be contacted through this site.

New members, who post their details, picture, and interests on the site, are listed on the day they join.

This kind of site is administered by volunteers, who are always ready with help and advice for newcomers.

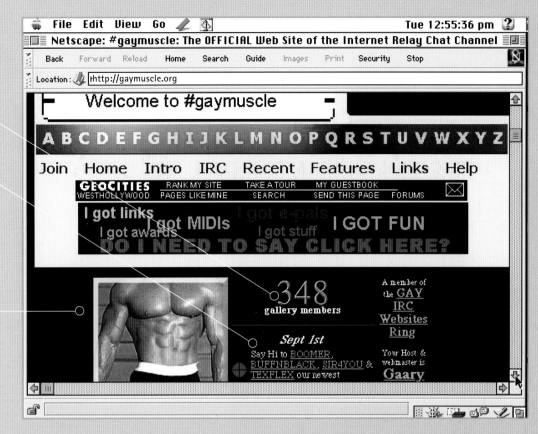

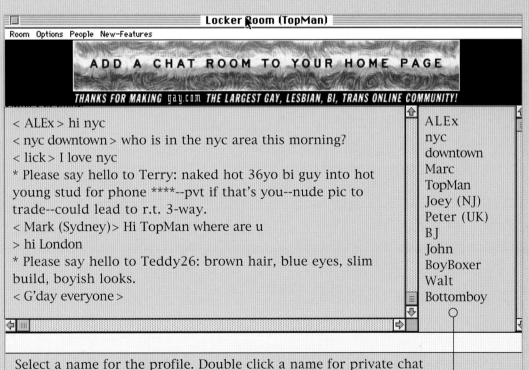

Select a name for the profile. Double click a name for private chat

From silent movie to wide screen

One-to-one video-conferencing is available if you have a computer-top video camera and Cuseeme, icuii, or Netmeeting software, but the screen is not unlike a security-camera video. Most computers do not have the memory to handle audio and video at the same time, so a text window is provided to chat.

Everyone can read what you type in the main window, or you can open a private window to chat with the user of your choice. The chat rooms hold a maximum of 30 users at one time.

DO YOU SPEAK INTERNET?

English is the *lingua franca* of international chat rooms, but standard English it most certainly ain't. Here is a selection of chat-room jargon to get you going:

As a "newbie" (first-timer), the first thing you have to do is decide your "nick" (the name you appear as in the chat room), which can be a real or assumed name or made up to indicate an interest or preference – for example, Sk8ter, LATop, Butt4U. When meeting for the first time, you may be asked for your "stats," a brief physical description, including any measurements you care to reveal or boast about, and asked for a self-pic – an on-line digital image of yourself that you can send in the bmp, jpeg, or gif picture file formats.

BUT IS IT ART?

FLAMING CREATURES

Shock tactics from the devastating Divine in independent filmmaker John Waters' Pink Flamingos *(1974).*

Since Stonewall, gay men have played an increasingly visible role in the arts, literature, and popular culture, both as creators and as subject matter. Gay artists and writers have been instrumental in shaping and defining the social, sexual, and physical identities that gay men have created for themselves, as well as reflecting them in their works. In the worlds of fashion, interior design, television, music, and film, gay men and women have also developed their own distinct styles.

Magic lanterns

Gay men's love affair with the movies long pre-dates Stonewall. Books such as Vito Russo's *The Celluloid Closet* (1981) reveal how many of Hollywood's leading directors, writers, actors, and producers were gay at the height of the star system in the 1940s and 1950s. Although they were firmly in the closet, these men helped shape the output of the Hollywood dream machine, and many more gay men packed out the movie theaters.

The first gay screen icons were not Hollywood's tough guys – John Wayne, Gary Cooper, and Clark Gable – but their leading ladies – the feisty Joan Crawford and Bette Davis, the vampish Jean Harlow and Mae West, and the tragically lost Marilyn Monroe and Judy Garland. Denied their own masculinity and marginalized by society, gay men of this period chose to identify with these larger-than-life screen goddesses, who symbolized both empowerment – as women who could hold their own in a man's world – and weakness – as women whose lives were marred by unhappy love affairs and self-abuse. Coincidentally, Judy Garland died a week before the Stonewall Riots, her death marking a symbolic closure of decades of submission to the established morality.

Stepping out of the celluloid closet

Post-Stonewall, gay men's relationship with the movies changed for good. The vocal, self-confident gay men in the 1970s had fewer reasons than their elders to be attached to the screen divas of the 1940s and 1950s. In the 1970s and 1980s, gay characters and themes slowly began to make their way onto American screens, though in Hollywood, these were largely negative images – two-dimensional queens or psychopathic misfits. In the bizarre *Cruising* (1984), Al Pacino plays a cop chasing a serial killer through the New York leather scene, and ends up a leatherman himself by some unexplained process of psychological transference. In the absence of commercial interest, it was left to independent American and European filmmakers, such as Andy Warhol (1930–87), John Schlesinger (1926–), Pier Paolo Pasolini (1922–75), Rainer Werner Fassbinder (1946–82), and Derek Jarman (1942–94), to investigate homosexual themes in a more direct and experimental manner. With a few exceptions, such as John Waters' anarchically subversive comedy *Hairspray* (1988), starring Divine, most of these films failed to reach global audiences because they lacked Hollywood backing and distribution.

MILDRED AND FRIENDS

Tragic heroine on and off screen Joan Crawford (below), Hollywood hard-woman Bette Davis (left), and the self-destructive Judy Garland (below left) were among the first generation of gay icons.

PA LAW

Philadelphia, *Hollywood's breakthrough HIV-AIDS movie.*

WE'RE NOT IN KANSAS

The first gay road movie, Australia's The Adventures of Priscilla, Queen of the Desert.

HIV-AIDS on the big screen

The breakthrough movie for tinsel town was *Philadelphia* (1993), starring Tom Hanks as a lawyer dying of HIV-AIDS while fighting a lawsuit against his employers for unfair dismissal. After *Philadelphia*, movies with gay themes were not only respectable, but also – much more significantly for the studios – good box office. However, Hollywood has made its fair share of mistakes, as the makers of *To Wong Fu, Thanks For Everything, Love Julie Newmar* (1995) discovered to their cost with their pale imitation of the Australian low-budget international hit *The Adventures of Priscilla, Queen of the Desert* (1994), which brought to the screen the adventures of three drag queens driving across the Australian outback from Sydney to Alice Springs. Much more successful with gay audiences was the low-budget adaptation of the off-Broadway play *Jeffrey* (1995), a comedy charting the soul searching of a young gay man during the height of the HIV-AIDS epidemic. In the 1990s, the commercial film industry in the United States still had an uneasy relationship with gay men and found comedy the easiest means of dealing with them, as in *The Birdcage* (1997), the American remake of the French classic *La Cage aux Folles* (1978). *The Birdcage* features Robin Williams as the owner of a drag club in South Beach who becomes embroiled with a right-wing senator, played by Gene Hackman.

SALAD DAYS

Another Country, the poignant tale of adolescent gay love in a British public school.

MARTYR'S CROWN

Art-house director Derek Jarman's Sebastiane explores modern gay themes in an ancient Roman setting.

SAINT DEREK

Derek Jarman was born in Northwood, a suburb of London, in 1942. He trained as a painter, graduating from the Slade School of Art in 1967, and took his first job as a set and costume designer with London's Royal Ballet. A master of light and color, Jarman made his first feature-length film in 1976, the classic *Sebastiane*, an idiosyncratic vision of Saint Sebastian's martyrdom that was shot in black-and-white and scripted in Latin. It was to be the first of many full-length and short films, which he managed to make despite his inability to raise funds from the mainstream film industry. In 1991 he was canonized by the Sisters of Perpetual Indulgence as St Derek of Dungeness of the Order of Celluloid Knights. He died of an HIV-AIDS-related illness in 1994.

Major films

Sebastiane, 1976

Jubilee, 1977

The Tempest, 1979

Imagine, 1984

Angelic Conversations, 1985

Caravaggio, 1986

The Last of England, 1987

War Requiem, 1988

The Garden, 1990

Edward II, 1991

Wittgenstein, 1993

Another country

In contrast, since the 1980s gay characters and themes have no longer been an issue in the British cinema. Positive gay characters and plot lines are common in mainstream movies, such as *Four Weddings and a Funeral* (1994), and British studios have scored a series of low-budget successes with gay-themed movies, starting with *Another Country* (1984), starring Rupert Everett as a gay public schoolboy, *My Beautiful Laundrette* (1985) starring Daniel Day-Lewis, and *Beautiful Thing* (1995), the bitter-sweet account of the coming out of two adolescents living in a London East End housing estate. French filmmakers, who delighted us with *La Cages aux Folles*, also produced the much darker *Savage Nights* (1992), an autobiographical account of director Cyril Collard's death from HIV-AIDS. The 1990s also witnessed the emergence of gay-themed films in Asia, South America, and Eastern Europe. In 1995, Nagasaki-born Ryosuke Hashiguchi (1962–) made *Like Grains of Sand*, a movie about a young gay man's love for his straight best friend. This was the first feature film with a positively drawn central gay character to be funded by a major Japanese studio. Often banned in their own countries, gay-themed movies from the developing world reach an international audience through international gay and lesbian film festivals, such as those held every year in London and San Francisco.

CALIFORNIA DREAMING

David Hockney was born in
Bradford, England, in 1937.
From 1959 to 1962 he
studied in London at the
Royal College of Art.
He was influenced by US
iconography and visited New
York in 1961. Three years
later, he moved to California,
where he produced his sun-
drenched "swimming-pool"
pictures. In 1974, the British
television documentary
A Bigger Splash (pictured
right) explored his
relationship with fellow
artist Peter Schlesinger.
Hockney became a member
of the Royal Academy of
Arts in 1991.

Major works and publications

*We 2 Boys Together
    Clinging*, 1961
Design for the opera
    The Rake's Progress, 1963
The Sunbather, 1966
*Six Fairy Tales from the
    Brothers Grimm*, 1970
Mr and Mrs Clark and Percy,
    1970–71
*David Hockney: My Early
    Years*, 1977
Design for the opera
    The Magic Flute, 1978
That's the Way I See It, 1993
The Studio March 28th, 1996

Still lives

During the long period of sexual repression in the
West, painting and sculpture were often the only
channels through which gay men could express
themselves with any degree of freedom. It is a
paradox that we owe some of the masterpieces of
Western art to the very organization that took the
lead in repressing homosexuality – the Catholic
Church. During the Italian Renaissance,
Michelangelo Buonarroti (1475–1564) painted and
sculpted his muscular fantasies to adorn the altars
and walls of the Vatican itself. While artists of genius have
often enjoyed more latitude in their personal lives than
other men, they, too, were restricted by censorship until
the post-Stonewall era.

Since the 1960s, gay artists have been increasingly free to
experiment with forms and subject matter. The range of work
and media is huge. The vivid yet tranquil paintings of David
Hockney (1937–) are in stark contrast to the tortured savagery
of Francis Bacon (1909–92) or the shock tactics of Gilbert and
George (1943–, 1942–), who have made their own lives an

ART OF LIVING

*London-based visual artists Gilbert
and George have made their life
together into a living artwork.*

DADDY OF THE MUSCLE ACADEMY

Tom of Finland was born Touko Laaksonen in 1920 in Kaarina, Finland. He moved to Helsinki at the age of 19 to attend art school. After a stint in the military during World War II, he began to work in advertising. He created his first homoerotic drawings for his personal enjoyment, and in 1957 he submitted them to the American magazine *Physique Pictorial*, under his now famous pseudonym. His images were an immediate success, and led to international commissions. With his friend Durk Dehner, he founded the Tom of Finland Company in 1979; the Tom of Finland Foundation was formed five years later as a non-profit educational archive to preserve and exhibit erotic art. In 1991, he was featured in the film documentary *Daddy and the Muscle Academy – The Art, Life, and Times of Tom of Finland*. He died later that year of complications from emphysema. The drawing shown on the left is from 1968 and features his leatherman hero, Kake.

artwork, and produce huge collages featuring shocking imagery that combines religious themes and alternative sexualities. Tom of Finland (see box, right), another master draftsman of the male form, needs to be mentioned here. Although he himself never claimed that his sexually explicit drawings of soldiers, sailors, and bikers were "art," they are now collected and exhibited by museums and galleries worldwide.

Snapshots

The male nude as subject matter is as old as photography itself. Blending the artistic with the pornographic, the form is now so well-established that the lavish, large-format tome of black-and-white nudes has become a standard of the publishing industry. Unlike their

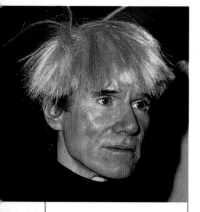

KING OF POP

The filmmaker and progenitor of Pop Art, Andy Warhol was born Andrew Warhola in Forest City, Pennsylvania, in 1930. After graduating from the Carnegie Institute of Technology in Pittsburgh, he moved to New York, where he worked as a commercial designer. He quickly became one of the lynch-pins of the New York art scene, working with various collaborators in the "Factory," as his studio-loft was called. He used the money from the sale of his art to embark on filmmaking. In June 1968 he was shot and wounded by Valerie Solanas, one of his starlets. He died in 1987.

Major works and films

100 Soup Cans, 1962
Green Coca-Cola Bottles, 1962
Blow Job (film), 1963
Sleep (film), 1963
My Hustler (film), 1965
Vinyl (film), 1965
Chelsea Girls (film), 1967
Flesh* (film), 1968
Lonesome Cowboys (film), 1968
Trash* (film), 1969
Frankenstein* (film), 1973
Dracula* (film), 1974

(* produced by Andy Warhol, directed by Paul Morrissey)

SNAPPING SEX

Photographers inspired by Robert Mapplethorpe have blurred the distinction between art and pornography in their depictions of the male nude. (Have and Take I by Robert Taylor, above.)

PICTURE PERFECT

The male nude is the theme of Blue, Australia's premier photographic glossy.

blue

barebacking: is not on in? | bob brown's coming out
sounds like queer radio | hot homebodies

JUNE 1999

№ 21

rufus wainwright | jean cocteau | washington dc

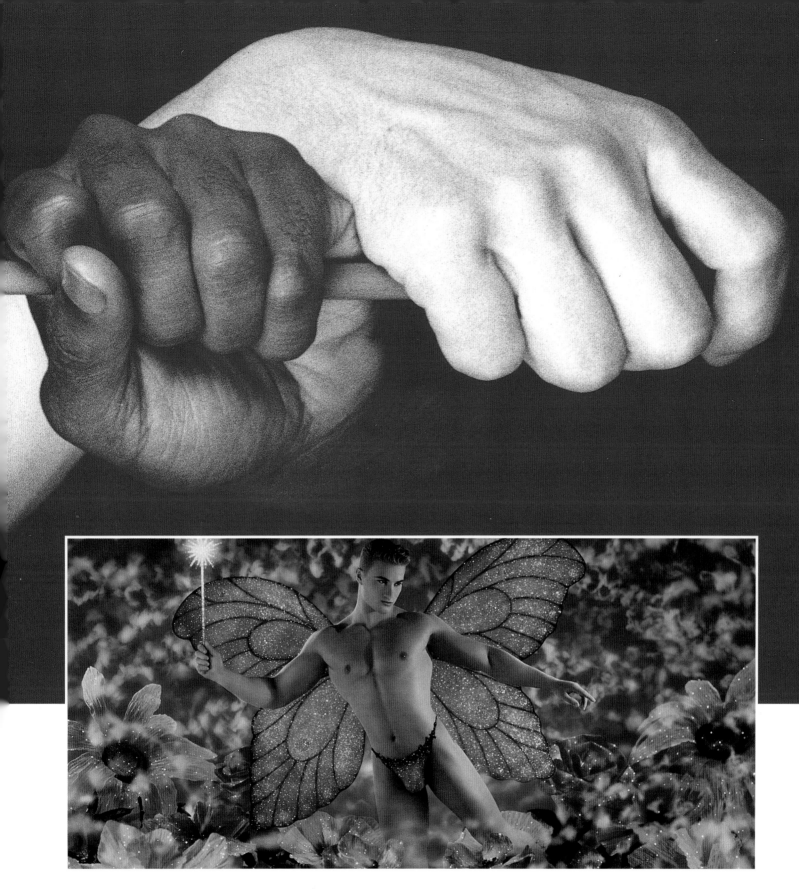

distant mentor, Wilhelm von Gloeden (1856–1931), photographers of the male nude have dozens of outlets for their work, such as the high-quality Australian photography magazine *Blue*. One of the acknowledged masters of the male nude is Robert Mapplethorpe (1947–89), whose provocative studies of sado-masochism still arouse controversy. More unusual are the icons of the French duo Pierre et Gilles, who have been inspired by popular Catholic imagery of the Virgin and saints. In the world of commercial photography, advertising and magazine photographers such as Herb Ritts and Bruce Weber have contributed to the creation of a gay aesthetic of the male form in their much-reproduced depictions of muscular men at work and play.

FLIGHTS OF FANCY

Fantasy becomes reality in the work of French photographers Pierre et Gilles. (Le Garçon Papillon – Kevin Meyer, 1993.)

Saturday-night fever

Although gay men's admiration of the Hollywood divas faded, it did not mean the end of their love affair with actresses and women entertainers. The gay icons of the 1970s were popular singers such as Barbra Streisand, Liza Minnelli, and Shirley Bassey, whose blend of sentiment and strength found a resonance in the gay community. However, at the end of the decade a new phenomenon – disco – changed the face of socializing forever. The glitz and glamour of the dance floor, dressing up, and the divas blaring out their anthems allowed gay men to escape the reality of their often troubled lives, and above all to feel that they had somewhere that was really their own. It was not long before they were packing out the mixed clubs, such as Studio 54 in New York and the Embassy Club in London. Within a few years, gay promoters were opening huge men-only venues, such as Heaven in London, Le Palace in Paris, and The Saint in New York.

The new idols of the disco cult were Madonna, Cher, Whitney Houston, and Kylie Minogue, who recognized that a large part of their audience was gay and gave them what they wanted. Gay male recording artists have been much less

SONGBIRDS

Taking up the torch from the Hollywood divas of the 1940s and 1950s, female recording artists such as Madonna and Cher (above right and right) were the gay icons of the 1980s and 1990s.

BOYS WILL BE GIRLS

Granddaddy of the gender-bending generation, Lou Reed (left), and one of his latter-day offspring, Boy George (above).

conspicuous and open about their sexuality. While a few have managed to flaunt their gender-bendering, defying the prejudices of the recording industry – Lou Reed and David Bowie in the 1970s, the New Romantics led by Boy George, Jimmy Sommerville, and Elton John in the 1980s – others, like George Michael, have stayed in the closet until outed by the tabloid press. In the 1990s, the new superstars of the music scene were not singers or even musicians, but DJs and club promoters, who set the lead gay tastes in music, fashion, drugs, and even travel, with the development of the party "Circuit" in the US and rave resorts such as Ibiza in Europe.

Gay's the word

Pre-Stonewall, a reader who wanted to read gay fiction had a stark choice: he could pick up a dog-eared anonymous porn novella in a sex shop or trawl through the literary cannon for the classics that dared breech the taboos of their age with descriptions of

same-sex relationships. In non-fiction, the reader's choice was even more limited: pseudo-medical and psychiatric texts, describing homosexual practices with a self-assured ignorance and bigotry that would be comic, had their consequences not been so tragic for the gay men and women of the period. A review of the gay fiction and non-fiction that has appeared since 1969 would quickly overflow the pages of this book and several more. Small gay presses were established in the US and Europe in the 1970s, taking advantage of the relaxation of censorship laws and the growing demand from gay readers. Their books were sold in a network of gay bookshops, such as A Different Light in New York, Le mot à la bouche in Paris, and Gay's The Word in London. In the 1990s, mainstream publishers finally recognized the potential size and profitability of the gay market and started their own gay lists, prompting the appearance of dedicated gay and lesbian sections in major bookstores. A series of anthologies of gay writing has been published since the 1980s by major publishers. A good starting point for anyone wishing to explore the rich and varied tradition of gay writing in the English language is *The Faber Book of Gay Short Fiction* (London and Boston, 1991), edited by Edmund White.

LET ME TELL YOU A STORY

*Gay storyteller extraordinaire,
Armistead Maupin (1944–).*

**TEN OUT OF TEN –
GREAT GAY WRITING**

James Baldwin
Giovanni's Room, 1956

Yukio Mishima
Confessions of a Mask, 1958

Jean Genet
Miracle of the Rose, 1965

Larry Kramer
Faggots, 1978

Armistead Maupin
Tales of the City, 1978

Edmund White
A Boy's Own Story, 1983

David Leavitt
Family Dancing, 1984

Andrew Holleran
Dancer from the Dance, 1986

Alan Hollinghurst
The Swimming Pool Library, 1988

Patrick Gale
Facing the Tank, 1989

Paper boys

If we use the *New York Times*' coverage of the Stonewall Riots as a guide, gays and lesbians, if they appeared at all pre-Stonewall, only existed as perverts to be belittled and condemned. Immediately after the riots, however, the first issues of campaigning gay papers and magazines were soon rolling off the presses. The American *Advocate* magazine had first appeared in September 1967, and was now

PUBLISH AND BE DAMNED

*The world's first gay press titles,
San Francisco's* Advocate *and
London's* Gay Times.

followed by Europe's first major gay publication, *Gay Times*, in the UK, the first of many political organs that continue to campaign vocally for gay rights and foster a sense of community among gays and lesbians. However, the most significant area of growth in the gay press of the 1990s was not in serious journalism or academic journals, but in that disposable lifestyle ephemera, the decidedly non-pc free papers and magazines that can now be found in every gay bar, café, and bookshop worldwide, which carry listings, scene and community news, and small ads. Many have developed from glorified pamphlets into weekly tabloids and four-color glossies, paid for by big name advertising, with circulations in the hundreds of thousands.

In the 1980s, the lifestyle magazine of choice for Western gays was the US edition of *GQ*, which was not shy of exploiting its unacknowledged gay readership with spread after monthly spread devoted to model Steve Aquilon in swimwear. Straight publishers Northern and Shell were the first to take the plunge in 1995 with the UK's first gay lifestyle magazine, *Attitude*, which proved to be an instant success.

Gay waves

Television in the United States has been even more restrictive than Hollywood in its treatment of homosexual themes. American networks in particular have been shy of offending their sponsors and advertisers with programming that might be seen as promoting homosexuality. There have been rare exceptions, such as Stephen, the gay character on *Dynasty*, but it has been left to lesbian comedian Ellen Degeneres to have the honor of being the first entertainer to break the ultimate taboo and come out on a network show. British broadcasting has been far more adventurous. Camp actors and stand-up comics, such as Kenneth Williams, Frankie Howerd, John Inman, and Larry Grayson, have been popular on both radio and television since the 1960s. In the 1990s, the hallowed BBC itself produced several series of *Gay Time TV*, a weekly gay current affairs and lifestyle show, as well as regular gay radio programming. Although several years behind Japanese TV, which broadcast its first gay-themed soaps in the

FIGHTING ON

Writer and activist Larry Kramer was born in Connecticut in 1935. His novel *Faggots*, published in 1978, defined a generation of gay America. A champion of gay rights, he was one of the founding members of both Gay Men's Health Crisis and ACTUP. In 1986, he wrote *The Normal Heart*, one of the first plays to dramatize the HIV-AIDS epidemic. He now campaigns to promote the positive depictions of gays and lesbians in the American media.

OVER TO YOU, BOYS

Ellen Degeneres, who broke the ultimate primetime taboo, is asking: "Will the male Ellen please stand up?"

CHRONICLER OF AMERICA

Edmund White was born in Ohio in 1940. After graduating in Chinese from the University of Michigan, he worked in publishing in New York. In 1983, he moved to Paris. A prolific journalist and chronicler of gay life in the United States (*States of Desire*, 1980), he also collaborated in writing *The Joy of Gay Sex* (with Charles Silverstein, 1977), and produced literary biography (*Genet*, 1993; *Proust*, 1999). His fiction includes the best-selling *A Boy's Own Story* (1982) and *The Beautiful Room is Empty* (1988). A collection of his best journalistic pieces, *The Burning Library: Writings on Art, Politics and Sexuality 1969–1993*, was published in 1994.

early 1990s, in 1999 Britain's independent Channel 4 produced the UK's first gay soap, *Queer as Folk*, which followed the lives of three gay men in the UK's second gay city, Manchester. In the 21st century, the explosion of digital, cable, and satellite TV channels, as well as broadcasting via the internet, is allowing gays and lesbians unprecedented access to the broadcast media.

Cocks in frocks

Many of the leading names of postwar fashion are famous fags: Gianni Versace, Yves Saint Laurent, and Thierry Mugler to name just three, but the high-priests of Paris and Milan *haute couture* and *prêt-à-porter* have traditionally concentrated their talents and energies on the more lucrative female market. In the 1970s, while the male models on the European catwalks sported stylish but conservative suits and casual wear, the field was left open to American designer Calvin Klein to take the first bite from the affluent gay urban male's wallet with his tailored preppy look. However, Klein's real claim to fame was his transformation of a baggy, invisible necessity into the ultimate gay fashion statement – designer underwear. By putting a man in briefs on a 100ft (30m) billboard in New York's Time Square, Klein broke every advertising taboo, and proved once and for all that

BUSTIN' OUT ALL OVER

French fashion guru Jean-Paul Gaultier (below), the man who put the "bust" back into the bustier, and the cock in a kilt.

flesh – male as well as female – sells. He and his legion of imitators now plaster magazines and billboards worldwide with acres of tanned male flesh bulging seductively in their figure-hugging briefs and boxers. The reaction to the preppy fashion of the 1980s was the grungy, fetishistic fashion of the 1990s, led from Paris by Jean-Paul Gaultier with his men's kilts, bondage harnesses, and rubber wear.

Cashing in on the body awareness of the gay community, hundreds of small fashion houses making sports and club wear have sprung up in the US, Australia, and Europe, but the first gay company to make a serious effort to break into the fashion big time with wares designed exclusively for gay men are the Tom of Finland Clothing Company, whose macho clothing with attitude is inspired by the drawings of artist Tom of Finland (see box, page 103).

Rainbow world

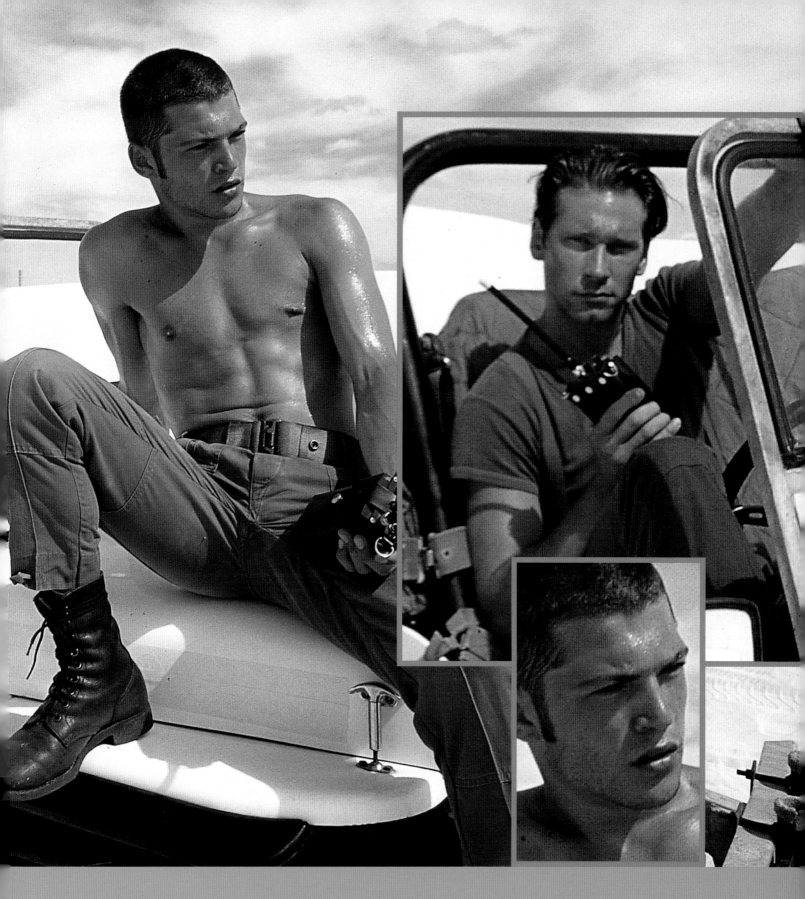

Gay men are natural-born travelers. Often uprooted in their youth by choice or circumstance, they are more than willing to embrace the new, the strange, and the exotic. There are very few places on earth worth going to that will turn away the gay traveler, because, as the old adage should have said: "Money talks ... every language!"

TRAVEL

Today, gay travel is a multi-billion dollar business, but in 1969 the gay tour operators, travel agents, hotels and guesthouses, holidays, and worldwide events that gay men now take for granted did not exist. A few gay men went to resorts such as Provincetown, Massachusetts; Fire Island, New York; Mykonos, Greece; and Gran Canaria, Spain, where they knew they would find a welcome or at least tolerance; or perhaps to cities known to have active gay communities, such as Amsterdam and San Francisco; or to countries whose cultures were more accommodating to homosexual practices, such as Thailand and Morocco. Nowadays, there are gay hotels, gay restaurants, and gay clubs in dozens of resort and city destinations. Gay travel companies that started as one-man operations in the 1980s have become major concerns, ferrying thousands of tourists to destinations worldwide, putting the pink dollar, pound, and euro firmly on the travel map. The range of gay holidays has expanded to encompass winter sports, cruises, and cultural and activity holidays, alongside tours to a mushrooming list of city and resort destinations. Whether it's opera in Milan or theater in London, gambling in Las Vegas or scuba diving off the Great Barrier Reef, leather in Berlin or hiking in Slovakia, whitewater rafting in New Zealand or cycling in France, there is a gay travel operator just waiting to turn your hard cash into solid gold memories.

THE GOOD SHIP LOLLIPOP: CRUISES

When 200 men boarded a liner bound for the Mediterranean in 1974, gay cruises were well and truly launched. Today, cruisers can choose from all-gay ships, hosted groups on such mainstream liners as Cunard's QE2, and private yacht charters. Cruises depart between September and March. The Caribbean and Mediterranean still top the list as most popular destinations, but up-and-coming ports of call include Alaska, Central America, and the Far East.

THE SLIPPERY SLOPE: WINTER SPORTS

If cruising at high speed with sheets of laminate strapped to your feet is your idea of heaven, then you're probably one of the thousands already taking advantage of the gay ski and snowboard weeks and weekends hosted by the world's leading ski resorts. The hottest cold spots in North America include Winterfest in Park City/Deer Valley (Utah) in March; Gay Ski Week in Aspen (Colorado) in late January, which includes a costume party that draws a 6000-strong crowd to the slopes; Canada's Whistler Gay Ski Week in late January to early February; and Gay Ski East in Lake Placid (New York State) in February. European ski resorts have followed suit with Gay Winterfest in Innsbruck (Austria) in March, Gay Ski Week in the Swiss Alps in March, and a yearly British-organized Gay Ski Week in the French Alps in March.

The Americas

Offering the widest range of vacations — from city breaks in New York and San Francisco, through Circuit parties in Palm Springs and Miami South Beach, to wilderness wanders in northern California — the US remains the world's prime gay travel destination. In Latin America, Rio's Carnaval and exotic beaches remain the biggest draw, but Cancun in Mexico and Buenos Aires in Argentina are both billing themselves as the places to go in the 21st century.

Eastern promise: eastern US

New York is a city for all seasons, but summer is the time to visit the three resorts of the north and mid-Atlantic states, where the big-city boys take their big-city ways to the beach. Proud of their pedigree as the first gay resorts in the United States, Fire Island (New York) and Provincetown (Massachusetts) draw huge crowds on weekends and to Circuit events, while late-comer Rehoboth Beach (Delaware) offers a homelier feel.

A bite out of the Big Apple: NEW YORK CITY (NEW YORK)

You've all been to Manhattan, New York City — even if you've never stepped foot in the US. No matter where you live or how old you are, you've been there in countless movies, novels, comics, and TV shows since childhood. Often, places you've seen so many times and heard so much about are a disappointment when you finally get there. They are somehow "lesser" or just different from what you imagined. However, New York ("so good they named it twice"), New York lives up to every single expectation and more. Whether you are cruising the avenues that form the north–south axes of Manhattan's checkerboard, in-line skating around Central Park, or just hanging out in the squares and circles, Sinatra's phrase: "If you can make it there, you can make it anywhere," really starts to make sense.

By the sheer size of its gay and lesbian population alone, the city has inherited San Francisco's title of "gay capital" of America, and most probably deserves the title of current world gay capital as well. It was here, after all, on the night of June 28th, 1969, that a group of gay men and women said "enough is enough," and

PRETTY IN PINK

*New York's famous landmark, the Empire
State Building, gets the lavender treatment
for Gay Pride.*

TIME OF YOUR LIFE

*Times Square ... whether as a visitor or a
resident, New York, New York offers a fast-
paced, high-energy lifestyle.*

fought back. Although they were not
the first to cry out against oppression,
their actions inspired a worldwide
movement. Fittingly, it is here, under
the pink-illuminated Empire State
Building, that men and women from
around the world gathered to
celebrate the 30th anniversary of the
Stonewall Riot in the biggest parade
and festival of gay, lesbian, and
transgender culture and diversity that
the city has ever witnessed.

New York City's high-energy
lifestyle is legendary. The sheer
concentration of money, talent, and
diversity should make it explode, but
somehow, it merely drives at break-
neck speed along the edge of the abyss.
Life in New York is the epitome of
urban gay life in the Western world –
it is not so much unique as just
"more." The city hosts its own Circuit

events (see page 135), the Black
and White parties, and, of course,
Pride. Its huge and ever-changing bar
and club scene can claim more than
its fair share of legends: Studio 54, the
Saint, the Roxy, Twilo, and Limelight,
in whose shadow have blossomed
hundreds of lesser and specialist
venues catering to every ethnic and
sexual diversity.

VILLAGE LIFE

The original hub of gay Manhattan,
Christopher Street in the West Village,
still thrives with gay-run shops,
restaurants, and bars, including the
re-opened Stonewall, but outside of
the big set-piece events, when the area
is invaded by hundreds of thousands,
the Village is quiet, catering for an
older crowd, and living up to its
name as a low-rise escape from the

high-rise, high-energy city around it. The beating heart of the city in gay terms has migrated north and east to the East Village and Chelsea. Here, a new generation of New Yorkers, most of them migrants from other parts of the US and from all over the world, have created a young, self-confident, exuberant urban culture with its own gyms, community organizations, restaurants, bars, and clubs. As has happened in many Western cities in the past decade, newly won freedoms and the fast pace of integration have meant the passing of the age of gay "ghettos" and the dissemination of the gay population throughout Manhattan and beyond into the neighboring boroughs and states.

Manhattan-sur-Mer:
FIRE ISLAND (NEW YORK)

If you have ever dreamed of being stranded on a desert island, cut off from such wonders of civilization as traffic jams, roads, and banks, then Fire Island just might be the place to indulge it, as long as your fantasy runs to playing Robinson Crusoe to several thousand Man-Fridays escaping the city in search of weekend R&R. During the May to October season, the island is connected by ferry to the port of Sayville on Long Island, itself an easy 80-mile (129km) train ride from New York. The island has two-dozen communities, but in gay terms, there are only two places to go: Cherry

Grove and the Pines. If you've only ever seen Fire Island in the pages of a magazine – which usually means the Pines – you might imagine that the large, fashionable houses are populated exclusively by A-list young, white, wealthy, gym-pumped urbanites, whose only concern is the size of their own and their prospective partners' pectorals.

However, there is a kinder, more relaxed side to the island in Cherry Grove. The homes of this older community are smaller, quirkier, and quainter, and often named with irreverent, camp humor. The Grove displays all the Big Apple's diversity, in terms of age, race, sex, income, and body type. Despite their differences, the two communities do exchange prisoners. Water taxis shuttle back and forth, ferrying the boys from the Pines to the Grove's better restaurants, and the Grove residents to the Pines' more intense nightlife. Another meeting point is the mile or so of forest that separates the Pines and the Grove – better known as the "Meat Rack" – which is high up in the Top Ten of North America's cruising grounds. The island's few bars and discos are usually packed, but the real social life goes on in private homes in a social whirl of lunches, dinners, and house parties. Finding a room on the island may be a problem because hotel and guesthouse accommodation is at a

BIG APPLE CHIC

Muscle boys and their admirers congregate in the café and bars of Chelsea, and hang around in the Village squares.

BEACH BOYS

In a yearly summer exodus, the gay population of New York heads to Fire Island to enjoy some sun and fun.

premium in these two tiny communities. Regulars organize a house share well in advance of the season (there are several options: full share meaning every week; half share meaning every second week; or quarter share meaning one week per month). Thomas, a young German Chelsea-ite, gives this glimpse of weekend life on Fire Island: "It's like being part of a big family. You are constantly in other people's houses for lunch and dinner. The atmosphere is carefree. People trust each other – you don't have to lock your doors there."

CARNIVAL CAPERS

On July 4th, the US celebrates its independence, and the streets of Ptown attract an international crowd of Circuit boys and their admirers to one of the biggest parties on the Atlantic seaboard. In mid-August, New England dresses up and coiffes its hair as Rio pays a visit to the north-east with a week-long carnival culminating in a costume parade complete with floats, carnival king, and, of course, plenty of carnival queens.

Cape of Good Hope:
PROVINCETOWN (MASSACHUSETTS)

Artists were the first to discover the charms of this small resort at the tip of Cape Cod, two hours' drive from Boston. Headed by playwright Eugene O'Neil, who came here at the turn of the century, the honor-roll reads like a *Who's Who* of American arts and literature: John Reed, Jackson Pollock, Edward Hopper, Mark Rothko, Truman Capote, Tennessee Williams, and Norman Mailer were all frequent visitors. By the swinging 60s, the Cape was a refuge for counter-culturists of all kinds, including a sizeable gay contingent. Today, along with Fire Island, it is one of the most visibly gay resorts in the US.

Staying in Ptown means a room in one of the 80 or so New England clapper-board guesthouses. Accommodation ranges from basic to chintzy, but don't expect a resort pool, jacuzzi, or restaurant in the guesthouse. The formula here is strictly bed and breakfast. Arising early for breakfast in or out, your first sunbathing and swimming option is at the social hub of Ptown, the Boatslip Beach Club Hotel, which has its own pool, sundeck, and beach access; however, you have to share the town beach with the Boston ferries and the fishing boats. The preferred option is to cycle or skate to the area's crowning glory, the 40 unspoiled miles (64km) of Cape Cod National Seashore on the Atlantic side. Remembering to pack a picnic, as this protected area has only one concession stand, follow the trail to Herring Cove and take a left toward Long Point, where you can enjoy an illegal nude sunbathe far from the families. It's a long walk, but the dunes and scrub behind the beach do provide a chance for a break if not a rest.

During the short official season that runs from Memorial Day (last weekend in May) to Labor Day (first weekend in September), the Boatslip hosts a daily tea dance at 3pm. Many start their drinking there, and unless they break for a spot of "retail therapy" in bustling Commercial Street, they continue steadily through the evening at the town's many bars and dance clubs, which close early at 1am. Revelers then head to Spiritus Pizza in Commercial Street to cruise, hang out, and try to be invited to one of the many private after-hours parties that go on until dawn.

Washington shores:
REHOBOTH BEACH (DELAWARE)

You won't find the Old-World clap-board charms of Massachusetts or the glitz and glamor of Miami South Beach in Rehoboth Beach. The ocean-front boardwalk is typical of a certain type of resort found all over the northern hemisphere. Tacky souvenir shops and amusement arcades jostle with fast-food outlets for the attention of families and day-trippers. Behind it lie the peaceful, suburban streets of small-town America, with its comfortable, modern low-rise homes. Despite the high year-round gay occupancy, there is still a perceptible tension between the straight and gay communities. So why is Rehoboth Beach the only gay resort of note between Fire Island and South Beach? Its selection is an accident of American geography and political history: it is two hours away from the nation's capital, Washington, DC. In the 1960s, it was far away enough from DC to be a safe haven for the gay politicos in fear of McCarthyite pursuit. The first gay resort, Renegades, opened in 1980 on the outskirts of town, and was quickly followed by bars and restaurants in the Baltimore Avenue and First Street district. Although the resort has not managed to land its own Circuit event, the gay beaches of Poodle Beach at the southern end of town and Cape Henlopen (North Shores) draw enthusiastic weekend crowds from as far afield as New York during the summer, as do the bars and regular Renegades party nights.

SANDY SHORES

The clapper-board charms of Rehoboth Beach are appreciated by summer visitors from the whole Eastern seaboard. Founded in 1980, Renegades (above and left) was the first gay-owned and operated resort to open its doors in the town; Poodle Beach (above right) becomes an oasis of prime gay flesh every weekend.

Some like it hot: southern US

The southern states of America have much to offer the gay traveler. Florida is the fastest growing state in the Union, and also the top gay winter-sin and sun destination in the world. Choose from three very different Florida resorts from November to April for an instant cure for your winter blues, but don't forget the jewel of the South, New Orleans, which beckons with its unique brand of French carnival excess.

Miami vice:

SOUTH BEACH (FLORIDA)

You do not go to SoBe (as Miami South Beach is called) for a relaxing vacation. For the legion of visitors who flock here, the miles of sun-drenched sand, the hotel pools hidden amid tropical blooms, and the beach-side cafés, bars, and eateries are merely incidental to the real reason for being here: to see and be seen. SoBe is a feast for the eyes, starting with the place itself. First developed in 1912, but demolished by a hurricane in 1926, this long spit of sand had its first boom in the late 1920s and 1930s, when many of the 800 hotels and houses of the Art Deco district were built to cater for an earlier generation of fashion-conscious sun-worshippers. Gays began to come to the area in the 1970s when it was still the domain of poor immigrant and retirement communities. The decades since then have seen the area entirely renovated, largely thanks to the efforts of gay and gay-friendly businesses. SoBe is unusual among gay resorts in the US because it is the only

DECO DREAMLAND

Restored to its former glory by gay business, the Art Deco district of Miami's South Beach is one of the United State's most stylish holiday destinations.

one close to a major city that has its own large and diverse gay scene and that is also home to large communities from Cuba and all points south. Transient and fast-paced, SoBe has never developed the strong sense of community that you will find in Ptown or Fire Island. In addition to the tourists who come for a week or two, the gay population is constantly shifting, consisting of thousands of seasonal workers who come from the northern US and Europe.

GET SOME WHEELS

A car is an unnecessary encumbrance in SoBe. The best way to see the sights is by the preferred local mode of transport: environment-friendly in-line skates. The time to set off is *après*-beach and gym in the afternoon.

Start by scouting the boutiques, galleries, cafés, and restaurants of the pastel-pink Lincoln Road Mall before you head south down Washington or Collins Avenues, lined with artfully renovated Art Deco hotels and condos. Hit the boy's beach by taking a left down 12th Street and then glide along to take in the parade of toned, tanned flesh on skates and bikes or just hanging out at the cafés on Ocean Drive. The beach is at its most pumped during the big set-piece events of the SoBe calendar: New Year and the Winter and White Circuit parties.

STARS IN THEIR EYES

A magnet for models, movie stars, singers, and their entourages of hangers-on and wannabes, SoBe has more than its fair share of both youth

and beauty. Put a lot of sexy, tanned hunks together, and you have a ready-made club scene. With owners such as Madonna and Prince, SoBe clubs have the muscle to attract the best DJs and the A-list crowd to the resort. Your evening out starts in the bars, the Twist being the local drinking institution, and then you can take your pick from a selection of permanent and weekly dance venues. With no work on Monday morning, no self-respecting SoBe clubber would miss the Sunday tea dance at Amnesia and an all-night session at Liquid.

CATCHING THE RAYS

If you're a sun-worshipper yourself, or just enjoy being in the midst of gleaming acres of tanned flesh, SoBe is the place to go.

Venice with palm trees:

FORT LAUDERDALE (FLORIDA)

If you prefer to dip into the SoBe scene but stay at a safe distance, Fort Lauderdale, 90 minutes north by car, is the mature alternative. The ocean-front provides all the amenities you'd expect from a resort, including several gay beaches, while the town behind it has a large settled gay community, with a club and bar scene with a more urban feel to it than SoBe, including the best bars that South Florida has to offer to the leather fraternity. A large part of the town is built on water, and as well as having cars in their garages, residents often have a boat docked at the end of their backyards. A trip on the water to one of the city's many waterfront seafood restaurants will take you past some of the most extraordinary mansions built by America's mega-rich.

Fantasy island:

KEY WEST (FLORIDA)

If you find Miami too young, star-struck, and frenetic, and your idea of a good time is lazing by the pool, drink in hand, with friends, then head for Florida's third major gay destination and the most southerly point in the Continental US, Key West. Here you will be welcomed by a large, settled, and much more sedate gay community enjoying the good life in this tropical paradise. The best way to get to the Keys is by driving along Highway One from Miami, which straddles the Atlantic Ocean and the Gulf of Mexico. The four-hour drive takes you over the ocean and through the other islands in the archipelago. With nightly thunderstorms out over the Caribbean, the drive rivals being

CONCH REPUBLICANS

Whether sunning yourself on "Dick Dock" or relaxing by the palm-shaded pool of your guesthouse, a stay in Key West will be a laidback experience.

serenaded in a gondola through Venice by moonlight as one of the most romantic trips on earth.

The island is small, so once you have checked into your guesthouse, park the car and hire a bicycle or scooter, or just set off for a stroll around the historic district of 19th-century "conch" houses. Gay guesthouses started to open here in the mid-1970s, and upward of three-quarters of the district owes its restoration to the hard work of gay businesses and residents. In Key West the next drink is only around the corner, but the main bar and restaurant scene is at the eastern end of Duval Street, which starts at the Gulf of Mexico and ends at the

Atlantic. Nearby the Atlantic end is "Dick Dock," which is a popular cruising spot both day and night. A more comfortable option for swimming and sunbathing is the deck of the restored Art Deco Atlantic Shores Beach Club, and for nature lovers, there is an intimate beach at Fort Zachary Taylor Historic Park.

There is an exciting calendar of gay events throughout the year – not that the eccentric residents of Key West need an excuse to put on the slap and dress up. However, they do so with particular relish in the last week of October, for the island's biggest party of them all, Fantasy Fest, the week-long celebration of "Conch Mardi Gras" better known as Halloween.

Southern Sodom:

NEW ORLEANS (LOUISIANA)

Few cities in the relatively young United States have preserved their historical heritage as well as New Orleans. To wander through the *Vieux Carré* (French Quarter) and Garden District is to discover the dangerous playground of the sybaritic vampires described in Anne Rice's *The Vampire Lestat*. The bars on Bourbon Street are always open, extending a warm alcoholic welcome to all-comers. The Big Easy's crowd-puller, though, is the Mardi Gras, held during the two weeks before Ash Wednesday. The celebration owes its origin to the Catholic tradition of feasting before the 40-day fast of Lent. Fat Tuesday itself is the traditional day for wearing masks, and the costumes are always elaborate. The "adult" Mardi Gras takes place in the French Quarter, where costumes can be more than revealing, and alcoholic excess encourages the traditional carnival chant of "Show me your (insert body part here)!" Honor-bound to comply, revelers expose themselves with impunity, as the police turn a blind eye on this day of days.

The lower French Quarter is the center for Gay Mardi Gras, and this is where you'll find the more extravagant costumes competing for a coveted Bourbon Street Award. The parade is on Fat Tuesday, and the town's secret societies, the Krewes, parade from early in the morning until late into the night. The first gay Krewe was founded in 1958, and by the 1980s they numbered in the dozens,

SHOWBOAT

Fat Tuesday's parade is the prelude to the night-long "adult" Mardi Gras held every year in New Orleans' frenetic French Quarter.

hosting gay balls that required the most outlandish "formal attire." Sadly depleted by HIV-AIDS, there are now only five Gay Krewes left: Amon Ra, Mwindo, Petronias, Armeinius, and the Lords of Leather. At 1pm every Mardi Gras, revelers head on over to Ambush Headquarters, 828 Bourbon Street, for the annual Krewe of Queenateenas Bead Toss. The bead toss is led by the Krewe's reigning King Cake Queen. For the best pearls on Bourbon Street, the rule is: you show, they throw.

VAMPING IT UP

Playground of Anne Rice's vampire Lestat, the Vieux Carré *retains its old-world colonial style.*

Home on the range: western US

City breaks in Los Angeles and San Francisco; Palm Springs, the Circuit capital of the desert; and Russian River (aka Walton's Mountain) make up a mixed bag of Californian delights for both winter and summer fun.

BLUE LAGUNA

When LA's urban charms pale, escape to the beach cities of Venice, Malibu, and Laguna Beach (pictured above).

City of fallen angels:
LOS ANGELES (CALIFORNIA)

If aliens were to land in the Greater Los Angeles area, they might conclude, after a cursory examination of the deserted pavements and packed freeways, that the local life-forms were obliged to live inside metal shells on wheels, like mechanized hermit crabs. In LA *Homo sapiens* has made way for *Homo mobilis*, and if you want to make the most of the city and its many attractions, your first stop should be at the car-rental desks at LAX. LA, like New York, is a place we are all familiar with from the movies and television, but unlike the gay metropolis of the East Coast, nothing can quite prepare you for its sheer size and chaotic sprawl. Los Angeles is not a city in the sense that residents of the older cities of Europe and the Eastern US understand the term. It is a city without a center; rather, it is a megalopolis made up from dozens of smaller cities and suburbs linked together by eight-lane freeways.

BY THE RIVERS OF BABYLON

While Hollywood has had some notable successes with gay-themed movies such as *Philadelphia* (as well as some memorable disasters: who could forget the *Priscilla* rip-off, *To Wong Fu With Love*?), to the casual outside observer the industry still looks hidden behind a half-open closet door. However, it has contributed in no small measure to gay rights by providing much of the funds for political campaigns in the US, as well as for the fight against HIV-AIDS. Historically, LA has been at the forefront of the gay liberation movement. In 1951, Harry Hay founded one of the pioneer gay rights organizations, the Mattachine Society, in Silver Lake. The 1960s saw the publication in the city of the *Advocate*, still America's most widely read "serious" gay and lesbian journal. On the spiritual side, too, LA has also led the way with the foundation in 1969 of the first gay church, the Metropolitan Community Church, which now has branches throughout the world.

TINSEL TOWN TRAVELS

For the gay visitor, coming to grips with the estimated half-a-million-strong gay community in a city with a population of over 15 million is not as daunting a task as it may first appear. The three neighborhoods with the highest concentrations are Hollywood, West Hollywood, and Silver Lake, with smaller outposts in the San Fernando Valley (aka "The Valley"), the beach cities, and in Central itself. The "gayest city in the world," the independent city of West Hollywood (aka WeHo), incorporated in 1983, is one of the few places in LA where you can be a pedestrian without feeling lonely. Gay businesses located there because it was outside the jurisdiction of the less-than-friendly authorities of Los Angeles and therefore free of police harassment. The strip on Santa Monica Boulevard between Robertson Boulevard and Fairfax Avenue contains the highest concentration of gay hotels, shops, coffee houses, bars, and clubs. The more rugged terrain of Silver Lake to the west of Hollywood is home to a large Hispanic-American community, and is naturally the center of the local Latino scene. With names such as Cuffs and Gauntlet II,

LIFE'S A DRAG

West Hollywood Muscle Marys showing off their assets. In Hollywood, city of illusions, nothing is ever quite what it seems.

you will guess that the area is also home to the local leather scene, which ranges from rugged to leather drag.

Los Angeles has more to offer the visitor than its rather soiled urban charms. To the south are the beach cities, Malibu and its stars, and Venice and its muscle beach. If you're after glitz, glamor, and gay, you can find them at the smart boutiques, galleries, and antique shops of Laguna Beach, 60 miles (96km) south of the city, where the well-heeled set goes for weekends by the sea. The desert is also nearby for those who want to escape to some of the world's most desolate landscapes. For lovers of the outdoors, the mountains offer a full range of healthy pursuits that are guaranteed to clear your head after the chemical excess of the LA scene.

Desert mirage:
PALM SPRINGS (CALIFORNIA)

Driving east from Los Angeles, you enter the extraterrestrial landscape of California's high desert. Here, you think, man must just be one more insignificant creature scurrying for shade in the 110°F (33°C) heat. As you catch sight of the lush Technicolor green of the gardens and golf courses of Palm Springs, however, you know that, even here, man reigns supreme. The 30 or so clothing-optional resorts of Palm Springs have been drawing crowds of sun-seeking sinners since the late 1970s. Uncompromisingly modern, comfortably furnished with the latest in hi-tech room amenities, spas, pools, and jacuzzis, they offer a heady mix of scenery, sun, skinny-dipping, and sexual excess. Many visitors never leave the confines of

WE LOVE MICKEY

The Disney Corporation was much criticized by the Christian Right for its equal employment policies for gays and lesbians, and a boycott of the company's theme parks and products was launched. Adding insult to injury, "gay days" were started at Disneyland in 1991, with happy crowds of 100,000-plus packing the Magic Kingdom from opening to Electric Parade.

EASTER PARADE

Circuit party king Jeffrey Sanker (above) organizes the Palm Springs White Party, one of the US Circuit calendar's premier events. (The three pictures shown on the right were taken at the 1999 White Party.)

their resort, but if the crowd is not entirely to your taste or you feel like a change, slip on your pants and try out the nighttime scene in nearby Cathedral City. The season lasts from November to April.

Tales of our city:

SAN FRANCISCO (CALIFORNIA)

Along with Amsterdam, Berlin, and, of course, New York City, San Francisco (or "The City," as the locals refer to it) is rightly remembered as one of the birthplaces of the modern gay liberation movement. Throughout the 1960s and 1970s, it drew thousands of young gay men from all over the US

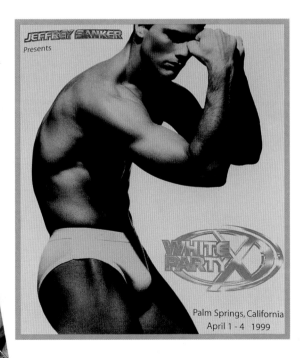

JEFFREY SANKER
Presents

WHITE PARTY X

Palm Springs, California
April 1 - 4 1999

WATERWORLD

Lost in the high Californian desert are the clothing-optional gay resorts of the verdant oasis of Palm Springs (right).

with a difference; and the social hot-spot, the Café Flore (aka "Café Hairdo"). However, gay life in today's San Francisco has moved far beyond the Castro and Polk Street into every part of the city. The gay community has come of age, and its former "ghettos" have been consigned to history and nostalgia.

ALL THE FUN OF THE FAIR

While the leather community suffered proportionally more from the AIDS-HIV epidemic that devastated the city's gay community in the 1980s, it is now thriving once more. One of the highlights of the San Francisco year, the annual Folsom Street Fair (in SoMa), is now the centerpiece of the Leather Pride Week in September, which sees the city taken over by thousands of members of the worldwide leather tribe. Starting at the Eagle, the length of the street shut off to cars and lined with stalls selling all things leather and offering tattoos and piercings, curious

OUR TOWN

The Castro, in San Francisco, the city of many gay firsts, is the spiritual home of the United States' gay liberation movement.

to the country's first visibly gay neighborhoods: Polk Street and then the Castro. San Francisco is a city of many gay firsts, and its battles were fought on the streets, in the bars and clubs, and finally in City Hall. The price of victory was often a high one. In 1978, gay activist and city supervisor Harvey Milk was assassinated along with gay-sympathizer, Mayor George Moscone. The lenient sentence given to their murderer triggered a riot in 1979 that cost the city US$1 million. This event is now marked by an annual march from the Castro to City Hall.

As one of the US's three major gay cities, San Francisco was hard-hit by the HIV-AIDS epidemic. For a second time San Francisco's gay and lesbian community led the fight, but this time against a very different adversary. The loss of so many innocent lives is remembered at the

Names Project in the Castro, where the AIDS Memorial Quilt (see page 69) originated, and in the annual Aids Candlelight March.

"WE'RE EVERYWHERE!"

To 40-something Brian, who was raised, like so many of the city's gay residents, somewhere else (Kansas City in his case), the Castro is one of the best reasons to live in San Francisco. He speaks of it warmly: "We have a community, a neighborhood to walk around in, to hang out in, to shop. There's really no other city that has anything quite like it " The Castro has certainly made the most of its reputation as the "queer capital" of the world. Your tour of the area's many attractions should include the Castro Theater, home of the International Lesbian and Gay Film Festival; Cliff's Variety, a hardware store, famed for its window displays

GOOD FOLSOM FUN

A yearly celebration of the leather lifestyle, Folsom Street Fair in SoMa.

TRAIL BLAZERS

The International Gay Rodeo Association (IGRA) is carrying the fight for gay rights deep into the heart of the Wild West.

SHORT CIRCUIT

Calendar of the main Circuit events:

Hearts Party (Chicago) *February*

Mardi Gras (Sydney) *February/March*

Winter Party (Miami SoBe) *March*

Black Party (New York) *March*

White Party (Palm Springs) *March or April (Easter)*

Gay Pride (NYC) *June*

July 4th (Provincetown)

Hotlanta (Atlanta) *August*

Folsom St Festival (San Francisco) *late September*

Black and Blue Party (Montréal) *October*

Halloween (New Orleans) *October*

White Party (Miami SoBe) *November*

New Year's Eve Party (Miami SoBe) *December 31st*

straight San Franciscans mingle with the leather community. The atmosphere is friendly and relaxed. City VIPs drop in for a courtesy call and pose for the photographers arm-in-arm with dominatrixes and boys in full bondage gear.

TEDDYBEARS' PICNIC

A reaction to the cult of the smooth, muscled Adonises of LA and New York, Bears, with their hairy chests and full beards, and Bearcubs (young hairy men) began to come out of the woods and organize in the mid-1980s. Spawning bars in SoMa and a magazine, aptly named *Bear*, they form a highly visible group with its own codes of behavior, sexual mores, and ideals, adding a new strand of diversity to this multi-faceted city.

BUCK AND RIDE

After shaky beginnings in 1976 as a charity fundraiser, Reno's gay rodeo was drawing crowds in the tens of thousands by the early 1980s. Spurred on by this success, gay rodeo groups appeared in quick succession in Colorado, Texas, California, and Oklahoma, leading to the foundation of the International Gay Rodeo Association (IGRA) in 1985. IGRA organizes a regular calendar of events, most of them west of the Mississippi. In addition to the spectacular rodeo fun and games, visitors can take part in square dancing, clogging, and Texas two-stepping.

Mountain men:
RUSSIAN RIVER (CALIFORNIA)

In complete contrast with the coastal and desert resorts of southern California, Russian River is northern

California's preferred gay resort destination. A 90-minute drive from San Francisco, the small communities of Guerneville, Forestville, and Monte Rio offer visitors the opportunity to relax, camp, hike, swim nude, and raft in some of the state's most spectacular scenery. The towns may be small, but the mind-set is anything but. Guerneville is the commercial hub of the area, and its bar and club would not be out of place in a big city. If messing around with tent pegs is just too much nature for you, you will find plenty of mountain cabins and riverbank cottages. The first gay guesthouses opened in the 1970s, and many offer heated pools, spas, gyms, bars, wholesome cheap eats, and views big enough to get lost in. The river is at its best in late spring or early fall to avoid the winter floods that have washed the town twice since 1984, and the heat of mid-summer. The season lasts from May to September.

MUSCLE MASS: THE CIRCUIT

Hi-energy music electrifies the room as lazers and spotlights sweep across thousands of bare-chested, entranced men, their muscular bodies so intertwined that it is difficult to tell where one begins and others end. Anyone who has been to a Circuit party will recognize this scene from the parties themselves or from the many official and unofficial parties that have sprung up to complement them. Today the Circuit spans the world, with events from Sydney to LA via Europe, attracting crowds in the thousands to the most diverse venues, which include beaches, hotels, and cavernous theaters and dance clubs.

Steve Kammon, editor of Circuit Noize *magazine, outlined what qualifies a party to be included in the Circuit: "The fact that people fly in for the party from around the world, the scale of the production, the venue, and finally that an internationally renowned DJ is flown in for the occasion. Of course, the real qualification is to be listed in the Circuit Schedule in the magazine!"*

The Circuit grew out of the yearly "Black Parties" held at the Flamingo in New York (later to become the Saint) and Probe in LA in the late 1970s. For the first time boys flew across the country to attend these events, and although attendance never reached the 1000 mark, they were a taste of things to come. The original Black Party was a members-only event. The US$100-a-year membership limited attendance to a self-selecting group who were older than today's Circuit boys and more into the leather scene. Sex was an important element of the event and often took place during the party.

HIV-AIDS hit the parties hard in the 1980s. Instead of sex, enjoying the event and music took over as the main draw. The Circuit today is not only younger and less interested in leather, but also more into physical appearance and much less sexual. In addition, the party drugs of the 1990s are designed for dancing and having a good time, but leave little energy for the physical act of sex once the night is over. Circuit events now typically take place over several days, with all the local clubs throwing supporting parties, pre-parties, and recovery parties.

Latin America

Beaches, carnivals, and salsa boys make the not-so-sleepy giant of Latin America one of the world's most sought-after gay destinations in the third millennium.

The boys from Brazil:

RIO DE JANEIRO (BRAZIL)

Author Martin Foreman summed up the joys of living in Rio with this story of a visit to an Ipanema supermarket. Taking his basket of groceries to the cash desk, he found himself standing in line behind one of the sexiest men he'd seen in his life. The only thing preserving the modesty of the young *carioca* (as the residents of Rio are called) was a skin-tight pair of white Speedos that beautifully set off his tan. "I never did find out where he kept his change," Martin said, his face glowing from the memory. Swimwear-clad

BARBIE TOWN

A tan, a smile, and a minute pair of Speedos is the national costume of the boys on Ipanema's Farme beach.

young men are a common enough sight in a beach resort, but in Rio, it is not only the sheer quantity and diversity that take your breath away, it is also because physical beauty is combined with a super-charged and quite unselfconscious sensuality that delivers exactly what it promises.

This vast megalopolis of 16 million people may suffer from huge social problems and inequalities, which are all too visible in the *favelas* (shanty towns) that share the city's beautiful mountainous site with the luxury beach condos and hotels of Copacabana and Ipanema and the ritzy downtown shops, but the *cariocas*, both rich and poor, have an irrepressible passion for life. Unlike their more conservative Spanish-speaking neighbors, Brazilians do not exhibit many inhibitions when it comes to

sex. On the contrary, they are never shy of taking full advantage of the many blessings of their mixed genetic inheritance and their tropical climate.

LIFE'S A BICHA

If Barry Manilow had set his song in Rio's rather than Havana's "Copacabana," his opening lyric might have been: "His name was Lola, he was a showgirl ..." Like other Ibero-American societies, Brazil has a historical tradition of transsexual and transgender lifestyles with a marked demarcation between *bofe* and *bicha* (butch and queen) roles. Egalitarian relationships are now much more common, but the unparalleled drag and male burlesque scene comes to the fore in the huge street party that is Carnaval. As you'd expect in a city with a population larger than many a

SUGAR LOAFERS

Leave your clothes and your inhibitions behind in the hotel when you take a stroll along the world's most famous stretch of sand, Rio's Copacabana beach.

small European country, Rio has many gay scenes, and sex is always available in movie theaters, baths, and from the many prostitutes advertising in the mainstream press.

For the tourist, the main areas are south of downtown in the beach districts of Ipanema, Copacabana, or Leblon, where you will find hotels ranging from the five-star luxury of the Copacabana Palace to budget hotels. The Palace is ideally suited for the gay section of the beach, the Bolsa, between *posto* 5 and 6. There, and on Ipanema's Farme beach, opposite the aptly nicknamed *Espelho Mágico* (magic mirror), a four-storey reflective glass building, you will find the "Barbies," as the local middle-class gym-bunnies are called, disporting themselves around the gay volleyball net. You will not have to go far for nighttime fun as these are also the main bar and club areas. On weekends crowds of up to 2000 descend on independent parties held in downtown warehouses and docks. Some of the most successful of these were the "Bitch" parties held in the 1990s in an amusement park in Rio.

THE WORLD'S BIGGEST STREET PARTY

To the outside world, Rio de Janeiro is synonymous with the largest outdoor party held anywhere on the planet, the yearly Carnaval when the whole city shuts down. The main event lasts for four days, but the parades and parties start two weeks before. Unlike Sydney's Mardi Gras, Carnaval is not a gay event, although gays are conspicuous participants and spectators as well as organizers. Not to be missed is the world's largest parade of drag queens, the samba parade itself on Sunday and Monday in the Sambadrome, the neighborhood bandas, such as the Banda da Ipanema, which strut their stuff on Fat Tuesday, and the dozens of gay carnival balls held all over the city, including the Scala Ball, the Sugar Loaf Ball, and the Grand Gala-Gay Ball.

Europe

The capitals of the European Union are long-established cultural and party destinations, but fast-growing in popularity are the capitals of the former Eastern bloc countries and Russia itself. Summer and winter options abound, but Spain's Mediterranean islands provide the only break from the cold European winter.

Northern Europe

Queer café-society enlivens the old-world charms of the northern cities by day, and intense dance cultures by night will ensure that you are well-and-truly "Euro-trashed."

Europe's gay capital:
AMSTERDAM (THE NETHERLANDS)

The phenomenal success of the 1998 Gay Games confirmed Amsterdam's reputation as the "gay capital" of Europe. For centuries, the Netherlands has welcomed political refugees and free-thinkers, and today, its social policies are among the most enlightened in the world. Amsterdam, nicknamed the "Venice of the North" for the canals that were once as congested with boats as the streets of other cities are with cars, is a charming old city built very much on a human scale. The main gay districts around the Warmoesstraat (near Central Station), Amstel, Reguliersdwarsstraat, and Kerkstraat are all within walking distance. A tour of Amsterdam would not be complete without a visit to Westermarkt's Homomonument, erected in 1987 as the city's memorial to the thousands of its gay citizens murdered by the Nazis during World War II.

You will find dozens of gay hotels and guesthouses all over the city, but for that once-in-a-lifetime experience, you can also rent a room on a gay-owned canal-boat hotel. Another boon for the Anglo-Saxon visitor is the faultless ease with which the Dutch speak English. Notable holidays on Amsterdam's calendar are Pride, held at the beginning of August, and Queen's Day on April 30th (note the apostrophe – it celebrates Queen Beatrix's birthday, not gays), during which the city is transformed into a gigantic street market by day and one long party by night.

Amsterdam doesn't have any no-go areas as far as gays are concerned, nor does it have a shortage of venues where you can meet and have sex with men in comfort and safety at any time of the day or night. If you cannot wait for the 10 or so dark rooms to open, and are not in the market for the brothels and escorts, then head for Amsterdam's sexual institutions, the Thermos saunas, probably still Europe's largest and busiest. The Thermos Day opens its doors from noon to 11pm, at which time the Thermos Night, several canals away, opens for business until 8am.

Leather heaven

The city's extensive leather scene centers on the bars and clubs of Warmoesstraat near the main railway station. Interrupted by the AIDS-HIV epidemic of the 1980s, the city's legendary kink and leather parties started up again in the 1990s, attracting regular crowds of 400 or more. The most popular events are organized by club promoter Trash and COC (Cultural and Recreational Center), as well as

some of the main bars. Once you've chosen your venue, make sure you meet the rigidly enforced dress codes: kinky, leather, uniform, and naked! If you have forgotten to pack your rubber chaps and leather harness, Amsterdam has some of the world's best and largest fetish and leather stores to kit you out for the night. The major leather events are Leather Pride, which was first held in the city in October 1996, and the Black Party, a European version of the party of the same name held in New York, which takes place on the Queen's Day weekend.

HELLO SAILOR!

One of the must-see sights in Amsterdam is Canal Pride, held during the Amsterdam Pride celebrations at the beginning of August. This spectacular event consists of a parade of decorated canal boats, crewed by Amsterdam's finest cruisers, which makes its way along the canals of central Amsterdam.

Black looks

Birthplace of Europe's leather scene in the 1950s, Amsterdam hosts a full yearly calendar of leather events.

CAFE SOCIETY

Amsterdam has become notorious in less tolerant parts of the world for its liberal attitude to drugs. You can buy and smoke ready-rolled, inexpensive joints in several gay-run coffee houses in the city. Visitors should note, however, that while Dutch law allows the possession of up to 1oz (30g) of marijuana for personal use, it does not sanction the use, sale, or possession of other drugs.

Life is a cabaret (reprise):
BERLIN (GERMANY)

The city that gave Liza Minnelli her
greatest acting role in *Cabaret* and
the world the Marlenes – Lili and
Dietrich – is not the largest gay city
in Germany, which is still Köln
(Cologne), but in the 21st century,
Berlin will certainly give the other
contenders for the title of "gay capital"
of Europe – London, Paris, and
Amsterdam – a good run for their
money. Berlin's gay community has a
long history. It was here in 1897 that
Dr Magnus Hirschfeld (1868–1935)
founded the "Scientific Humanitarian
Committee" (WHK), the first
organization that campaigned for
the abolition of laws against
homosexuality. In the roaring 20s,
Berlin was one of the few cities in
Europe to have a visible large-scale gay
community with its own meeting
places, among them the El Dorado in
Motzstrasse, which was visited by
Marlene Dietrich and was a source of
inspiration for Christopher
Isherwood's *Goodbye to Berlin*. The WHK,
which had several branches in other
European countries, survived until
1933 when, along with the city's
gay culture, it was extinguished
by the Nazi Holocaust. The death
of 100,000 German homosexuals
is commemorated at the
Nollendorfplatz U-bahn station by a
plaque in the shape of the pink
triangle that they were made to wear.

GERMANIC JESTS

*Carnivals and pageants have been held in
Germany since the Middle Ages, a tradition
taken up by German gays in their yearly
Christopher Street parade.*

RISING FROM THE ASHES

At midnight on October 3rd, 1990, the Freedom Bell of the Schöneberg town hall rang out over Berlin, signalling the reunification of East and West Germany. The process has often been a painful one, both economically and socially, but for gay Germans from the former Communist DDR, who were prevented from traveling to the West in the days of separation, it came as a joyous moment of liberation. A symbol of a reunified Germany, Berlin is once again the country's capital with a gleaming new parliament built within the shell of the old Reichstag building. In an elegant full circle, the WHK founded by Magnus Hirschfeld was reborn in 1998.

Berlin has a large, self-confident, and highly visible gay scene, with hundreds of shops, saunas, cafés, bars, clubs, and community organizations in the Schöneberg, Kreuzberg, and Prenzlauer Berg districts in the center of the city. The scene is so varied that if it exists,

WILLKOMMEN, BIENVENUE, WELCOME!

Joel Grey camps it up in pre-war Berlin in the 1971 movie Cabaret.

then it's available in Berlin, whether its vanilla, leather, kink, fetish, indoor, or out. If you travel to the eastern side of the city, through what used to be known as "Checkpoint Charlie" in the days of the Berlin Wall, you will still be able to notice some differences, but hurry because these

are fast disappearing as the city is torn down and rebuilt. The major events to attend in Berlin are the Motzstrasse Street Fair, which takes place in early June, and the Christopher Street Parade held on the Saturday closest to June 27th, which is Berlin's own tribute to the Stonewall Riots.

TOGETHER AGAIN

The Brandenburg Gate, Berlin, the symbol of the new united Germany.

NO SEX, PLEASE, WE'RE BRITISH!

Britain decriminalized homosexual acts between consenting adults over 21 in private as early as 1967, yet it has been slow to allow sexual activity in the kinds of public venues that exist in countries with far less liberal statutes. This began to change in the 1990s, with the opening of dark rooms, saunas, and cruise clubs all over the city. Although these remain technically illegal, they owe their continued existence to changing attitudes to sex and promiscuity in the wider community and a realistic approach by the police.

Cool Britannia:
LONDON (GREAT BRITAIN)

There are two cities in the world where you can go out clubbing on Friday night and party without a break until the following Monday morning. The first is New York and the second is London. The two cities vie for the title of dance capital of the world, trading musical styles, DJs, and club fashions, sometimes moving to the same beat, sometimes drifting apart. London started to swing in the 1960s and has never looked back. Its vast and fast-changing club scene caters to every age group and every conceivable musical taste and sexual preference. Heaven, London's answer to New York's Saint, opened as Europe's largest gay club in 1981, and is still going strong after a major facelift in 1998. Alongside the permanent venues, there are dozens of weekly and monthly club nights, as well as one-off specials coinciding with England's public holidays. While many of these are in the West End, London's theater and commercial district, you will also find small clubs in outlying districts, including the venues catering to London's active fetish and ethnic scenes.

FROM THE WEST TO THE WEST END

If you had visited London in the 1970s and 1980s and wanted to see the action, you would have been directed west from the center to Earl's Court. Here, gay life went on behind the shutters of rather gloomy Victorian pubs and in discreet basement dance clubs. Penetration of the Soho district of the West End, where there had been an underground gay presence in

private members' clubs since the pre-war period, was slow, but it picked up pace in the 1990s. The area was once a sleazy ghetto of straight brothels, porn shops, and strip joints, but a city-sponsored clean-up operation, and the appearance of a new style of gay establishment – cafés, restaurants, and bars open to the street and visibly gay – transformed Soho's main drag, Old Compton Street, and the surrounding blocks into today's lively 24-hour "café society" on the European model. Soho's businesses host an annual street party in September, the Pink Weekend, with a small parade complete with floats. If you still hanker after a visit to a traditional British pub, there are plenty left in the suburbs. Another great British pub tradition, drag, is alive and swinging its handbag nightly at venues such as the Black Cap in Camden, north London, or south of the river at the Royal Vauxhall tavern in Vauxhall.

LONDON NIGHTS

The party capital of Europe offers a dizzying variety of bar and club venues to suit all tastes.

TRADE

During the 1990s, clubbing in London was synonymous with this one-nighter at Turnmill's in London's Clerkenwell district, a 10-minute cab ride to the east of Soho. The creation of promoter Laurence Malice, Trade opens at 4am on Sunday morning and closes at 1pm. Both winter and summer, the queues stretch around the block, but the impatient clubbers continue to find Trade's mix of sweaty muscle, hard techno, and "altered" states completely irresistible.

Belle de nuit:
PARIS (FRANCE)

The French capital is a magnificent stage-set of neo-classical palace, square, and arcades and Art Nouveau façades ranged majestically along wide tree-lined boulevards. Amid all this, modernity has been skilfully interspersed, creating the surprising architectural paradoxes of the Marais–Les Halles, the Arc de Triomphe–La Défense, and the Louvre and its famous pyramid. Compact in size, this extravagantly beautiful aristocratic landscape has for centuries been the playground of gay men.

In the City of Lights, cruising has always meant a lot more than sailing down the Seine in a *bateau-mouche*. The city's streets and open spaces offer endless possibilities for the adventurous visitor – the *grands boulevards*, the parks near the Champs Elysées, the Tuileries Gardens, and most famously, the *quais* along the Seine, re-christened "Tata (queen's) Beach" for part of its length, where men go to sunbathe on hot summer days and to stroll on all but the coldest nights.

LA VIE EN ROSE

Paris may be the capital of romance, but it also has a down-to-earth approach to sex. Saunas have operated all over the city since the 1970s. In the 1980s, these were complemented by bars with back rooms and later "cruising" clubs, whose number steadily increased in the 1990s. In a way, this tolerance of such discreet, private places for gay encounters, combined with a rigid Catholic, conservative environment, retarded the appearance of the city's gay community as a visible, organized force. This changed in the 1990s with the dramatic increase of participation in Gay Pride events, which reached 120,000 in 1997, the year Paris hosted the pan-European Europride. Another reason for increased visibility was the creation of a gay quarter in the center of Paris. In the postwar period, gay men used to frequent the elegant sidewalks and cafés of the Boulevard Saint Germain on the Left Bank. Upstairs at the Café de Flore, made famous by such luminaries as Jean-Paul Sartre, was a popular meeting place for fashionable gay Parisians until the 1980s. As in many other cities, gay businesses identified an area ripe for redevelopment. In Paris, this was the Marais, close to the commercial heart of the city and Les Halles, and the arts complex of the Centre Pompidou. In the streets of this ancient quarter, you will discover the full range of *cafés-terrace* and restaurants, shops, and bars.

LEFT BANKERS

Take a break from shopping, sightseeing, and cruising to sunbathe on "Tata Beach" on the banks of the Seine in the center of Paris.

FRENCH CAN-CAN

Paris is famed as the capital of fashion, not only in clothing but also in nightlife – bars and clubs have to re-invent themselves continually to keep their appeal. The fast-changing club scene began in the intimate, dressy, and expensive clubs of the rue Sainte Anne in the Montmartre district, and spawned larger clubs, such as the Palace, with its VIP basement, the Privilège, in an old theater in Montmartre. This has now closed its doors, as have many venues of the 1980s and 1990s, but the Queen still thrives in its unparalleled location on the Champs Elysées, while young entrepreneurs create new venues in previously unvisited districts of the city, such as République and the suburbs.

Southern Europe

The sun-baked coasts and islands of the Mediterranean offer a wide range of summer vacation options from May to September: city breaks in northern Italy and Spain, party madness on the Balearic island of Ibiza, and mellow moments on the Greek islands.

Viva Catalunya:
BARCELONA WITH SITGES (SPAIN)

When you arrive in Barcelona, you are left in no doubt that while the city lies within the borders of Spain, it is also the capital of the autonomous province of Catalonia. Newspapers, TV, and radio, and the flyers you will be given for bars and clubs, will more often than not be in Catalan rather than Castillian Spanish. Close to the French border, the region has a rich cultural heritage and its own language, both of which were savagely repressed during the dictatorship of General Franco. The end of the fascist regime in 1975, and the accession of the democratic King Juan Carlos to the restored Spanish throne, brought liberation to both the provincial minorities in the country and to its gay community.

The coast around Barcelona has long been a popular destination for tourists from northern Europe, and the 1992 Olympics confirmed the city as one of Europe's leading cultural and economic centers. The north-east of the Iberian peninsula is blessed with an extremely mild climate, allowing the Catalans to lead a great deal of their lives outdoors. They are great after-dinner promenaders, and the *paseo*, which means a walk around in the evening with nothing particular to do but to see and be seen and meet friends, occasionally stopping for a coffee or a drink at a sidewalk café, is a Spanish institution. Every major city has a square or thoroughfare set aside for the *paseo*. In Barcelona, it is along the broad central pavement of one of the city's great arteries, the Ramblas, where you can watch mimes perform, listen to musicians, buy souvenirs and snacks from hawkers, and, of course, cruise to your heart's content. So when in Barcelona, do as the Catalans do and just let yourself be led by the crowd. You will quickly meet someone who will take you to the cafés and bars frequented by gays around the Ramblas, or lead you on an exploration of the many venues in Eixample behind the university.

LIFE'S A PLAYA

In July and August, Barcelona is baked by the relentless Mediterranean sun, and even its wide tree-lined boulevards and parks become airless and oppressive. Fortunately, there are several beaches (*playas*), including a nudist beach, all well-frequented by the gay community, within the city limits. On weekends, however, the locals flock to the nearby beach resort of Sitges. A popular holiday destination in its own right, the town is a 30-minute train ride from central Barcelona. You can go for the day on Saturday or Sunday, but arrive early if you want a lounger and a parasol, because the gay section of the beach in town is small and gets packed early. There are also two nudist beaches, the Playas del Muerto, a little way out of

BARCELONA BABES

One of Europe's economic hotspots, and Spain's fashion and style capital, Barcelona attracts a steady stream of gay tourists to its bars and beaches.

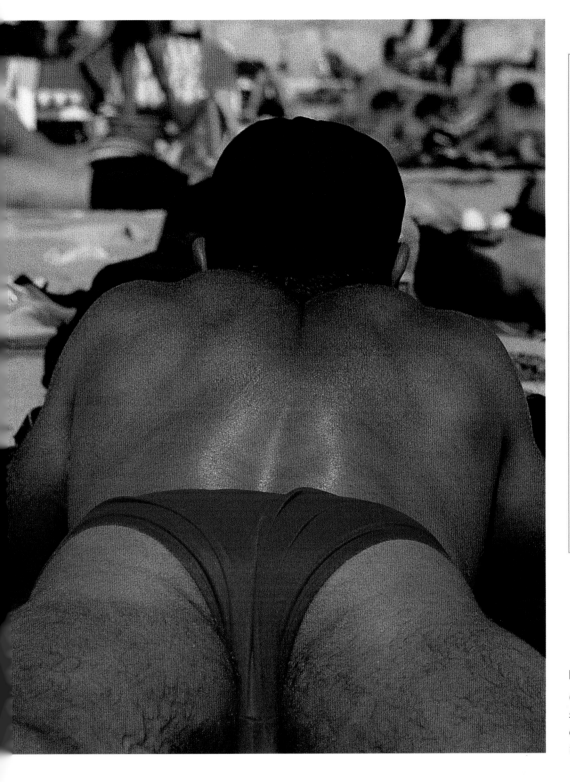

CARNIVAL

Carnival traditions continue all over Europe, and gays have not been slow to spot them as an opportunity to throw a good party. One of Europe's wildest carnivals is held in February in Sitges. The highpoint of the week-long celebrations is the "death of the king of carnival." In an updated version of an ancient ritual, the king dies because he has overindulged in drugs, sex, and alcohol. His last will and testament is read in the main square, and he is then paraded through the town in his coffin attended by a procession of bejeweled drag queens dressed in black fur coats. The procession ends at the beach where, to the accompaniment of a magnificent son et lumière show, a man dressed as the devil springs from the ocean and burns the coffin on the beach.

BOTTOMS UP

Cheek-to-cheek on the small gay section of the beach in Sitges proper ... or take a hike 2 miles (3km) out of town to the nudist Playas del Muerto.

town with the obligatory and conveniently placed pine forest behind them, but even with a car they are quite a trek along rocky paths. If you opt to stay in Sitges for a few days, you can choose one of a dozen or so gay hotels or rent a more economical self-catering apartment. During the day, the town is full of families and straight tourists, but as the sun sets, the boys come out to play. A late dinner at one of the many gay restaurants (though they may be a bit expensive for the budget traveler), many with outdoor seating in gardens and courtyards, is the best way to start the evening. Then on to sample the lively nighttime scene, although you are more likely to meet French, Italians, English, and Germans than Spaniards in its bars and dance clubs.

DO YA WANNA DANCE?

The cult island of Ibiza is the home of Europe's biggest and best summer party scene.

Cult island:
IBIZA (SPAIN)

Ibiza, like all Mediterranean resorts, hits its peak in July and August, the months that coincide with the most dependable weather, and summer vacation time for students and northern Europeans in general.

It is possible to have a quiet romantic time with a partner on Ibiza, but to do so you'll have to go there in May or September, which also have the more bearable weather. Ibiza is a large and varied island, which has been heavily developed in recent years. German, Scandinavian, Dutch, French, and British holiday developments ring the island's coast, and you'll have to travel inland to find any trace of traditional Balearic village life.

Unless you're planning to hire a car, there is only one place to stay on the island, in Ibiza old town itself, preferably inside the city walls, or in the nearby district of Figueretas, which has its own gay-friendly beach. In the traditions of all long-established gay beaches, the island's main gay beach at Es Cavalet is a bus ride from Ibiza town, followed by a healthy 15–20 minute walk through — you guessed it — a pine forest. Packed during high season, the beach has a concession stand that blares out dance music. If contemplating crowds of boys lounging around in sarongs or in the nude is not your scene, or you want a more private place to enjoy with a new friend, there are plenty of quiet coves and smaller beaches in the vicinity.

THE DAILY ROUND

An evening out in Ibiza follows a well-established pattern. Back from the beach in late afternoon and rested or worked out, you will dine late at one of the trendy open-air eateries in the old town. Rather than going to the busy establishments on the main streets, wander through the winding alleyways of this medieval town where you will chance upon the more *recherché* establishments hidden in small courtyards and back alleys. Fortified, you are ready for the walk down to the bars strung along the length of the splendidly misnamed Calle de la Virgen that runs parallel to the sea front. As the evening wears on, patrons make their way back toward the old town, some to the bars and the only dance club, the Anfora, others to enjoy the view and the company on the quieter section of the well-preserved city walls.

The island's party scene, which has made Ibiza famous across the globe with both straight and gay clubbers, goes on through the night in large mixed clubs outside Ibiza town. The original Amnesia and Ku, which were huge open-air venues, have either closed or been roofed because of noise restrictions. Their successors, the Privilege and Space, are vast hangar-like spaces with several dance floors, bars, and pools. British promoters, such as Manumission and Trade, draw huge crowds at their regular parties in July and August.

Island shopper:
GRAN CANARIA (CANARY ISLANDS, SPAIN)

You are more likely to hear German and English than Spanish spoken in Playa del Inglés and its sister city, Dunas de Mas Palomas. Located on the southern coast of the Spanish island of Gran Canaria, the resort is Europe's one and only gay winter-sun destination. An archipelago of a dozen small islands off the African coast settled by Spain in the 15th century, the Canaries are twice blessed: by nature, because of their year-long temperate climate; and by man, because of their status as a tax-free port. You do not go to Playa del Inglés for its quaint Spanish charm. The resort is a product of the 1960s tourist boom, which has left it a legacy of ugly high-rise blocks and large undistinguished shopping centers. A short cab ride from Playa del Inglés is Mas Palomas, still very much "a work in progress," a city of low-rise holiday resorts built in Spanish or Moorish styles to cater specifically for northern Europeans.

TAKE A WALK ON THE WILD SIDE

While self-catering is the cheapest option if you plan to visit the resort of Playa del Inglés, an increasingly popular choice for visitors to Gran Canaria are the gay-owned and operated resorts in Mas Palomas. Many visitors opt to spend the daylight around the resort's pool drinking duty-free alcohol like it's going out of fashion, but if you do make it to the beach, which is nude, you will immediately notice how seamlessly the gay and straight holiday-makers are integrated.

The gay section is in the middle of the beach, which stretches for several miles fronting the 810 acres (328 hectares) of the Dunas Nature Reserve. Although you can take a bus to the beach, the effort of the 30-minute trek through the dunes to the seashore will be rewarded by some interesting "sites," not just the extraordinary dunes themselves, which are up to 30ft (9m) high, but also because the park is a naturist area much favored by sun-starved northern Europeans.

IN THE HEAT OF THE NIGHT

Whether you are staying in the resorts of Mas Palomas or in Playa del Inglés, evening means a trip to the Yumbo Center. This huge open-air shopping center loosely modeled on a Minoan palace is the heart of the nighttime scene. Built on four levels around a broad open plaza, the center contains, in ascending order, a sauna, a bookstore, cafés and restaurants, bars, leather cruise bars and cabarets, and dance clubs. In the early part of the evening, as the straight shoppers and family tourists begin to retire, gay men meet for drinks or coffee on the center's lowest level. Cabaret and drag, in English and German, wile away the hours until it is time to go to the bars on the uppermost level. The half-dozen establishments are set out in a horseshoe shape, and by unspoken agreement, the patrons move slowly from one to the next, taking full advantage of the low prices charged for generous measures. It is gone 1am when it is time for the general exodus down and across the plaza, where one side of the second level is lined with bars, cruise clubs, and dance clubs where the party continues until dawn.

NATURE WATCHERS

The stunning sand dunes of Mas Palomas are a nature reserve and nudist area.

Greek gods:

MYKONOS (GREECE)

Far from the hustle of gray, polluted city streets, there are places only ever seen in travel brochures, where clear blue skies meet cobalt blue waters, and stepped white villages hug golden shores. However, the small Greek island of Mykonos is one such place for real. Although it is only a 30-minute flight from Athens, if you have the time to spare and want to reset your internal clock to the infinitely more laidback Mediterranean rhythm, take the ferry from Piraeus for the seven-hour cruise to the island.

Mykonos may not have the historical cachet of the Greek islands of Santorini, Rhodes, or Crete, but for the summer months, it becomes the home of a constantly regenerated

colony of visitors from Greece, northern Europe, and beyond, who come for their week in the sun. By luck or foresight, Mykonos has escaped the depredations of the holiday complexes and high-rise condos and hotels that disfigure so many western Mediterranean resorts. Here, the houses and hotels are built in the local style, with flat roofs and whitewashed walls, though furnished with up-to-date facilities. Self-catering is a popular option, but there are plenty of luxury hotels and more reasonable guesthouses to satisfy every budget.

This is not a place to be in a hurry. The cobbled streets wind anarchically, opening up into small picturesque plazas. As a first-time visitor, you will get lost until you learn to recognize the major landmarks. The beaches are a little way out of town, and the best gay beach, Super Paradise, is a bus ride to Paradise Beach and then a boat trip if you are not up to the 15-minute walk along the cliffs. The town has lively bars and a mixed out-of-town club scene, but despite its efforts to join the Circuit with the Twelve Gods Party in September, this is still an Ibiza or SoBe wannabe. The season is from May to September.

LOTUS EATERS

For a laidback summer break, the island of Mykonos offers tranquil beaches and whitewashed village streets.

Asia-Pacific

The mysteries of the East have always drawn gay men to Thailand, Japan, and the Philippines, but these countries' gay cultures remain hidden to prying foreign eyes. On the other hand, Australia and New Zealand are a home-from-home for Anglo-Saxons in search of summer pleasures.

The original Boyztown:
BANGKOK AND PATTAYA (THAILAND)

Like the smile on the face of the giant Thai Buddhas, this southeast Asian country remains enigmatic for foreign visitors. This ancient culture has long traditions of homosexuality and male prostitution. This cannot be written off as the product of a colonial past because Thailand is the only country in the region that escaped foreign domination in the 19th century. Thailand is a country that challenges not only our expectations but also our assumptions about what it is to be gay. Bangkok has two very different faces: one for visitors from the developed world who flock here for sun and "sex tourism," and the other, the largely inaccessible Thai gay scene. You will not see many Thai men in the boy bars of Bangkok during the high-season from December to May, though the manager of one establishment, a former boy himself, assured me that they would visit at other times.

Without a mass-transit subway system, Bangkok has the dubious honor of being one of the most congested and polluted cities on the planet. Getting around this over-crowded, sweltering, and seasonally flooded city (avoid the monsoon season from September to October at all costs) can be quite a challenge, and if you are a nervous passenger, steer clear of the motorized rickshaws that weave at break-neck speed through the traffic jams. The city offers a wide range of accommodation, from the back-packers' hostels to the Western hotels around the Sukhumvit Road and in Patpong, the surreal heart of the gay and straight sex industry, where you will also find the boys bars, saunas, and massage parlors, which apart from sex, also offer suitably strenuous Thai massage.

Without the stigma found in other cultures, traditional Thai prostitution developed into a large-scale international sex industry. Sadly, this has contributed to a nationwide HIV-AIDS crisis of catastrophic proportions, which this poor country has limited resources to alleviate. Fortunately, the Thai government woke up to the scale of the epidemic in the 1990s and has been taking measures to promote HIV-AIDS awareness among sex-industry workers. In 1999, Thailand began trials of an AIDS vaccine in collaboration with its American manufacturer.

TROPICAL DRAG

Two hours' drive from the crowded, pungent streets of Bangkok is the beach resort of Pattaya. Once a sleepy Thai fishing community, the town was chosen as an R&R spot for American GIs fighting in the Vietnam War. The rest, as they say, is history. Today's Pattaya is an international resort with comfortable modern high-rise hotels and Western restaurants. There are two gay areas in the resort, to the south, between Beach Road and Second Road. Here you can enjoy nightly open-air drag and cabaret acts under the tropical skies, which are popular with both straight and gay tourists. You can also sample the local talent in a handful of bars in the northern area of the resort between Tanon Neua and Soi See.

AN EVENING OUT WITH THE BOYS

The lights dim, the music increases in volume, and the spotlights flood the stage at the far end of the room, revealing two elfen-faced, oiled muscle-boys in jockstraps, who look as if they are in their teens but are more likely to be in their early 20s. For the next 30 minutes, they and other boys put on a show that spans the full sexual range from "vanilla" to S&M. The show's purpose is to persuade the customers to part with their hard cash. The boys on stage and in the bar, all minimally clad in jocks, Speedos, or shorts, have a badge with a number for easy identification. The club will receive a payment for hiring out the boy, and then it is up to you to agree a price with him – all fees are completely negotiable. Rooms may be available on the premises, in a nearby sex hotel, or you may choose to return to your own hotel. The boys, who mostly come from the poorer provinces, work as prostitutes for several years, saving enough money to set themselves up and marry.

The wizards of Oz:
SYDNEY (AUSTRALIA)

For the many visitors from Europe and North America who flock here in March like migrating birds to attend the world's premier queer event, the Gay and Lesbian Mardi Gras (see pages 46–47), Sydney is definitely the "Emerald City" of the southern hemisphere. With all the social and cultural amenities you'd expect to find in a major Western city, the capital of the state of New South Wales not only has some of the most enlightened legislation protecting gays and lesbians and people suffering from HIV-AIDS from discrimination, as well as immigration rights for same-sex partners, it is also ringed by stunning beaches and enjoys a year-round sub-tropical climate, with skin-baking hot winters and mild summers. All the various strata of big-city gay life are represented: from leather to drag, via 30-to-40-something professional muscle boys; a large contingent of sex-industry workers, mostly in their late 20s and many of whom work part-time; and the very young, whose styles range from feral to "*nouveau hippie*" and beyond. The large Asian-Australian gay community has also started to organize its own bar spaces and scene.

THE GOLDEN MILE

Originally located in the King's Cross district, now a sleazy strip of run-down bars and amusement arcades, the gay community migrated to the quaint Victorian charms of the residential districts of Darlinghurst, Paddington, and Surry Hills. The "Golden Mile," the busy commercial Oxford Street, is the local equivalent of the WeHo strip in LA. It is not just place names such as Paddington and Oxford Street that make the English-speaking visitor feel that he is home from home in Sydney: gay bars are called "pubs" and share many features with their British equivalents, with plentiful supplies of beer and nightly drag.

Pubs are primarily a place to meet friends and socialize rather than cruise. The city's licensing laws forbid sexual activity of any kind in pubs, and this led to the emergence of a diverse and thriving sauna and sex-club scene in the 1980s. These have remained open throughout the HIV-AIDS crisis thanks to the local gay community's strong pro-sex gay response.

PARTY TOWN

Partying in Sydney is very much geared around big set-piece events. Apart from Mardi Gras itself, there is a string of smaller but similar functions, which provide a focus for a wide cross-section of out-and-about Sydney gays of all ages. These include the Sleaze Ball, the sell-out Mardi Gras fundraiser in November, which many claim is an even better party than the main event in March, the Hand in Hand party in June and Pride at New Year, both of which draw 10,000-plus, and the Leather Pride party, which attracts a healthy crowd of 2000.

BEACH BALLS

A visit to Bondi Beach to inspect its lifeguards and surfers is a must, but only on your way to Sydney's real local seaside hotspot, Tamarama Beach, nicknamed "Glamorama" because of the acres of bronzed, oiled, meticulously groomed gym-bunnies posing in the briefest of bathing costumes on its white sand or paddling among its very impressive breakers. Tamarama is friendly and social – a good place to get to know the locals and find out what's going on. On the other side of town you'll find the popular and isolated rocky outcrops of the nudist Lady Jane Beach.

A NIGHT AT THE OPERA

Whether you're a culture vulture, party animal, or sun-worshipper, Sydney has something to offer the discerning winter visitor (bathing in view of Sydney Opera House, left).

EMERALD CITY

Many gay men have been tempted to apply for permanent emigration to Australia, so that they can enjoy this gay haven all year round.

Africa

The tip of the Dark Continent is a little less dark since the promulgation of South Africa's model constitution.

MANDELA'S BABES

Cape Town, the party capital of Africa, has a warm welcome for all-comers, regardless of race, color, creed, or dress sense (Cape Town Pride, 1998).

Out in Africa:
CAPE TOWN (SOUTH AFRICA)

Until the end of *apartheid*, the racist policy of the white-minority governments, South Africa was an unlikely destination for gay tourism; it remained *terra incognita*, despite its many areas of outstanding natural beauty, its resorts, and its unmatched wildlife reserves. Repressive legislation kept the local gay community underground until the mid-1990s, when the promulgation of the new constitution, the first in the world outlawing discrimination on the grounds of sexual orientation and guaranteeing freedom of sexual association, transformed the country into one of the world's top gay winter-sun destinations and led to the establishment of an immigrant gay community in search of the good life. All the major South African cities have developed lively and highly visible gay scenes, and none more so than that of the oldest Western city in sub-Saharan Africa: Cape Town.

CITY OF MANY COLORS

Straddling the Indian and Pacific oceans and dominated by the mighty Table Mountain, Cape Town is worth the visit for the dramatic beauty of its site alone. Bathed in delicious summer sunshine while those in the northern hemisphere endure the yearly big freeze, Cape Town's high season is December, January, and February. However, visitors start arriving in the quieter late fall and stay until early spring. Like the Dutch capital, Cape Town is a favored destination of New Age travelers (or "tee-pees," as they are known to the locals), who come to bathe in the mystic energy of Table Mountain, usually under the influence of the extremely potent plant-life that flourishes on its slopes.

The city on the Cape has always been one of the most cosmopolitan cities in South Africa, with large "colored" (as people of mixed parentage are called here), white, and black communities. While complete integration between the groups is still a little way off, the gay scene is a heady mix of blond, blue-eyed Afrikaners, Blacks, Indians, Malays, and "English" South Africans.

While you are likely to meet gay men in any part of the city, you will find the main area of restaurants, cafés, bars, and clubs to the east of the city bowl in Green Point, which is undergoing considerable redevelopment. The club scene is seasonal, reaching its peak in mid-summer. Isolated for so many years for geographical as much as for political reasons, the South African gay community is particularly welcoming of foreign visitors, who will not find it difficult to join in the active social life that revolves around visits to the beach and *braaivleis*, the South African for barbecue.

THE GREAT OUTDOORS

Gay men, long denied their own public spaces in which to meet, have a strong tradition of outdoor cruising. In Cape Town, this includes the city's many gay beaches – but a word of warning: the cold current on the Atlantic Ocean side makes the water so cold that it will cool any bather's ardor and seriously shrivel his prospects! However, the scenic beauty of the beaches at Sandy Bay, Camps Bay, and Clifton, and the flesh on display sunning itself on the nudist sections, more than make up for the coolness of the water. If swimming and water fun is your thing, you can go to the Graaffspool, a men-only nudist tidal swimming pool, or travel an hour or so to the warmer Indian Ocean side to Gordon Bay. For both car and pedestrian cruising, the busiest spot is the stretch of road between Green Point and Sea Point in the early evening and again after the clubs have closed.

Index

Credits

Quarto would like to acknowledge and thank the following for supplying pictures reproduced in this book:

(key: *l* left, *r* right, *c* center, *t* top, *b* bottom)

p2 Michele Martinoli; p6 Trip; p7*br* C Moore Hardy/Gaze; p8 Bill Short/*Gay Times*; p9*r* Robert Workman/Gaze; p10 Image Bank; p11*t&b* Image select; p12 Sylvia Corday; p13 Image Select; p14*t* Ron Volanti Jr; p15 Trip; p16 Image Bank; p17 Robert Workman/Gaze; p18*tl* courtesy of JS Enterprises, *b* Gordon Rainsford/Gaze; p19*t* Sunil Gupta/Gaze, *b* Paul Vallance/Gaze; p20 Paul Vallance/Gaze; p21*t* Stuart Linden/*Gay Times*; p22*t* Australian Tourist Commission, *b* Brad Roser; p23 The Ronald Grant Archive; p24 Anne Bungeroth/Gaze; p25 Gordon Rainsford/Gaze; p26 Image Bank; p27*t* Image Bank; p28 Image Bank; p29*t&b* Sylvia Corday; p30 Trip; p31 Paul Miles/Gaze; p32 Michele Martinoli; p33 The Ronald Grant Archive; p34 Paul Vallance/Gaze; p35*tr* Lola Flash/Gaze; p36 The Ronald Grant Archive; p37*tl* Robert Workman/Gaze, *tr* Image Bank; p38 Sharon Wallace/Gaze; p39 Image Bank; p40 Lola Flash/Gaze; p41 Sunil Gupta/Gaze; p42 Geoff Manasse/Gaze; p43 courtesy of the US House of Representatives; p44*b* Sharon Wallace/Gaze; p45*t&b* Gordon Rainsford/Gaze; p46 Australian Tourist Commission; p47*t* Australian Tourist Commission, *br* Piers Allardyce/Gaze; p48 Hinter Wipflinger/Gaze; p49 Hinter Wipflinger/Gaze; p50 James & James/Gaze; p51 Michael Skipper/Gaze; p52 Laura Salisbury/Gaze; p53 *M with RT Torso* © Robert Taylor; p54 Steve Mayes/Outrage; p55 Steve Mayes/Outrage; p56 The Ronald Grant Archive; p57 Image Bank; p58 Geoff Manasse/Gaze; p59 Sharon Wallace/Gaze; p60*t&b* Annie Bungeroth/Gaze; p61 Geoff Manasse/Gaze; p62 Tom McKitterick/ Impact Visuals; p63*t* Image Bank, *bl* courtesy of The Terrence Higgins Trust, *bc&br* courtesy of GMFA; p64 Trip; p65 Tom McKitterick/Impact Visuals; p66*tl* Gordon Rainsford/Gaze, *tr* Ron Volanti Jr, *br* Capital Pictures; p67 Gordon Rainsford/*Gay Times*; p68*t* courtesy of GMFA, *b* Paul Vallance/Gaze; p69 Trip; p71*tr* Trip; p72 *Le Fumeur de Narquilé – Aziz* 1996 © Pierre et Gilles/courtesy of Galerie Jerome de Noirmont; p74 *Bob McCune* 1958 © Bruce of Los Angeles/courtesy of the Tom of Finland Foundation; p75*tr* Image Select, *br* Robert Raylor/Gaze; p76*tl* The Ronald Grant Archive, *b* Eric Chaline; p78 Trip; p79*tr* Gordon Rainsford/Gaze, *bl* Fred Malmgren; p80 courtesy of Mancheck.com; p81*tl* Capital Pictures, p81*tr* Robert Taylor; p82 The Ronald Grant Archive; p83 Robert Taylor; p84 Robert Taylor; p85*tr Paratrooper* 1994 © IΩN/courtesy of the Tom of Finland Foundation, *bl Take* © Robert Taylor; p86*tl* courtesy of Zipperstore, *br* Dixie Thomas/Gaze; p87*bl* Michele Martinoli, *cr* courtesy of Zipperstore; p88 *Slave* 1995 © Kent/courtesy of the Tom of Finland of Foundation; p88*tl* The Ronald Grant Archive, *tc* Uncut Kurt for Expectations, *tr* courtesy of International Mr Leather, *b* Michele Martinoli; p90 Eric Chaline; p91*tr* Ben Delil/Riedijk Productions, *b* Michele Martinoli; p92*bl* courtesy of *Zipper* magazine, *br* courtesy of *OG* magazine; p93*tr Steam* 1997 © Kent/courtesy of the Tom of Finland Foundation, *b* courtesy of *Honcho* magazine; p94 The Ronald Grant Archive; p95 courtesy of Prowler Press Ltd; p98 The Ronald Grant Archive; p99*t,bl&br* Image Bank; p100*t&b* The Ronald Grant Archive; p101*t&b* The Ronald Grant Archive; p102*tl&b* The Ronald Grant Archive, *tr* Piers Allardyce/Gaze; p103*t* 1968 drawing courtesy of the Tom of Finland Foundation, *br* Phillip Stuart/courtesy of the Tom of Finland of Foundation; p104*tl* Capital Pictures, *bc* Michele Martinoli/courtesy of *(not only) Blue* magazine; p105*tr Have and Take I* © Robert Taylor, *b Le Garçon Papillon – Kevin Meyer* 1993 © Pierre et Gilles/courtesy of Galerie Jerome de Noirmont; p106*bl* Andy/courtesy of Trade, *tr&br* Capital Pictures; p107*tl* Capital Pictures, *tr* Gordon Rainsford/Gaze, *br* Image Bank; p108*tl* Gordon Rainsford/Gaze, *bl* courtesy of *The Advocate* magazine, *br* courtesy of *Gay Times* magazine; p109*bl* The Ronald Grant Archive, *tr* Gordon Rainsford/Gaze; p110 Bill Short/*Gay Times*; p111*t* courtesy Calvin Klein, *br* Piers Allardyce/Gaze; p114 Sarah Booker/Gaze; p115*tr* Travel Ink; p116 Image Bank; p117*t* Trip, *br* Moira Clinch; p118 Sylvia Corday; p119*t,b&c* John Addy/*Gay Times*; p120*l* Chuck Anzalone; p121*t,c&b* Tricia Massella/CAMP Rehoboth; p122 JW Shank/Gaze; p123 Image Bank; p124 Matt Oxley/Gaze; p125 Justine Buchanan/Gaze; p126 Trip; p127*t* Moira Clinch; p128 Trip; p129 Paul Miles/Gaze; p130*bl,bc&br* courtesy of JS Entreprises; p131*l* courtesy of JS Enterprises, *r* Matt Oxley/Gaze; p132 Trip; p133*tl* Sunil Gupta/Gaze, *br* Ron Volanti Jr; p134 Trip; p135 Martin Labelle/BBCM Foundation, event organizer of the Black & Blue party in Montreal; p136 Trip; p137*t&b* Trip; p138 Trip; p139*t* Hinter Wipflinger/Gaze, *b* Gordon Rainsford/Gaze; p140 Suzanne Jansen/*Gay Times*; p141*t* The Ronald Grant Archive, *b* Image Bank; p142*l* Annie Bungeroth/Gaze; p143*l&r* Gordon Rainsford/Gaze, *tr* courtesy of Trade; p144 Paul Vallance/Gaze; p145 Paul Vallance; p146 Travel Ink; p147 Sunil Gupta/Gaze; p148 Trip; p149*l* Bill Short/*Gay Times*, *r* Trip; p150/151 Sarah Booker/Gaze; p152 Image Bank; p153 Trip; p154 C Moore Hardy/Gaze; p155*l&r* C Moore Hardy/Gaze; p156 Paul Miles/Gaze; p157 Trip

All other photographs and illustrations are the copyright of Quarto. While every effort has been made to credit contributors, Quarto would like to apologize should there have been any omissions or errors.